Dr. Alicia Holland's
Starting and Operating an
ONLINE TUTORING BUSINESS:
The Blueprint for Running an Online Learning Organization

2nd EDITION

Book Titles by Dr. Alicia Holland

Dr. Alicia Holland's
Becoming a Better Tutor:
A Data-Driven Approach to Tutoring

Book 1:
Expanding Your Tutoring Business:
*The Blueprint for Building a
Global Learning Organization*

Book 2:
Expanding Your Tutoring Business:
*The Blueprint for Hiring Tutors and
Independent Contractors*

Book 3:
Dr. Alicia Holland's
Expanding Your Tutoring Business:
*The Blueprint for Protecting
Your Learning Organization*

Dr. Alicia Holland's
**Starting and Operating an
Online Tutoring Business:**
*The Blueprint for Running an
Online Learning Organization*

*Note: Check Dr. Alicia Holland's Personal Website
for her latest work at*
www.dr-holland.com

Starting and Operating an
ONLINE TUTORING BUSINESS:
The Blueprint for Running an Online Learning Organization

2nd EDITION

Dr. Alicia Holland, Ed.D

All rights reserved. No parts of this book may be used or reproduced by any means, graphic, electronic, or mechanical, including photocopying, recording, taping or by any information storage retrieval system without the written permission of the author except in the case of brief quotations embodied in critical articles and reviews.

This book may be ordered through booksellers or by contacting:

iGlobal Educational Services, LLC
PO Box 94224
Phoenix, AZ 85070
www.iglobaleducation.com
512-761-5898

Because of the dynamic nature of the Internet, any web addresses or links contained in this book may have changed since publication and may no longer be valid. The views expressed in this work are solely those of the author and do not necessarily reflect the views of the publisher, and the publisher hereby disclaims any responsibility for them.

Dr. Alicia Holland's Starting and Operating an Online Tutoring Business: The Blueprint for Running an Online Learning Organization

Copyright© 2017 Alicia Holland, EdD. All Rights Reserved.

ISBN-13: 978-1-944346-57-7

Dedication

This book is dedicated to those who have entered this profession seeking to make a difference in their clients' lives both academically and personally. You are very bold and selfless to share your knowledge with the rest of the world and serve as a merchant of hope to individuals who need help with their learning needs.

Georgia, Amaiya, and future children, this book is also dedicated to each of you and to your future success.

Table of Contents

How this Book is Organized..ix
Introduction 1
Acknowledgments 3
My Assumptions 5

**PART I: The Early Stages of Planning
   Your Online Tutoring Business**............................7
   Chapter 1: Introduction to the
   Fabulous World of Tutoring................................ 9

   Chapter 2: Becoming a Legitimate Online
   Tutoring Company... 25

**PART II: Establishing and Promoting Your
   Online Tutoring Business**.........................43
   Chapter 3: Selecting an Online Tutoring Platform............ 45

   Chapter 4: Organizational Needs for
   Your Online Tutoring Business 57

**PART III: Applying the Lesson Framework and
   Building an Online Curriculum for
   Your Tutoring Business** 83
   Chapter 5: Applying the Dr. Holland-Johnson's
   Lesson Framework. 85

   Chapter 6: Building a Customized Online
   Curriculum... 89

PART IV: Data-Driven Tutoring in the Virtual Classroom 97

Chapter 7: Conducting Online Tutoring Sessions and Writing Monitoring Notes for Clients 99

Chapter 8: Determining the Type of Tutor You Will Need to Be for Each Tutoring Session 135

References *151*

About the Author *152*

Index *154*

How this Book is Organized

Dr. Alicia Holland's *Starting and Operating an Online Tutoring Business: The Blueprint for Running an Online Learning Organization* is organized into four major parts—the following sections explain what you will find in each part.

Part I: The Early Stages of Planning Your Online Tutoring Business

In this section, I introduce you to the fabulous world of tutoring. You will discover why tutoring is in high demand and who can enter the tutoring profession. I discuss all of the necessary steps to legitimize your online tutoring company so that you can do business. You will have an opportunity to assess your start-up needs and learn how to properly budget for projects. In addition, I talk about the importance of selecting a business name, logo, and corporate identity package that will promote your company's brand. You will find that building an online business is similar to launching a physical tutoring company.

Part II: Establishing and Promoting Your Online Tutoring Business

The chapters in this section discuss selecting an online tutoring platform, effectively attracting clients, and organizational needs for your tutoring business. Just because you are providing online tutoring, it does not mean that all online tutoring platforms are created equal. As a result, you need good information to determine which platform works best for your online tutoring business. I provide guidelines to help you select a platform that will enable your clients to get the best results in the virtual classroom.

You will have an opportunity to explore the various marketing strategies to promote your tutoring business and start a website. There is a myriad of marketing strategies that can be used, but in this part, you will learn the best approaches to use for your tutoring business.

Lastly, you will learn about how you can find online clients and how to work with new and returning clients. I provide step-by-step details on how to implement my 13-step process for working with both new and returning clients. After reading this chapter, you will definitely be equipped to provide both data-driven instruction and quality customer service to your clients.

Part III: Applying the Lesson Framework and Building an Online Curriculum for Your Tutoring Business

Before planning a tutoring session, it is important to focus on components of an actual tutoring lesson plan. In Part Three, I discuss how to apply the Dr. Holland-Johnson's Lesson Framework. You will explore ten components that will help you better understand how the lesson framework for effective tutoring. You will then explore some questions that will help you build your customized online curriculum.

Part IV: Data-Driven Tutoring in the Virtual Classroom

In this part, I discuss how to develop instructional plans for your clients, conduct online tutoring sessions, and write monitoring notes for clients. Once you have determined the client's needs, you need to determine the type of tutor you will need to be. Therefore, I discuss various tutoring prototypes and how they are used in tutoring sessions.

Introduction

This book is very much needed in the tutoring industry as many learners are opting to receive instruction online or in the virtual classroom setting. In response to this demand, tutors need to have a blueprint that will help them build a quality online tutoring program.

This book has been created for the independent tutor or learning organization who desire to work with students online. My seminal work on tutoring, *Becoming a Better Tutor: A Data-Driven Approach to Tutoring*, has been well received since its first publication in 2010. In addition to my seminal work, I have authored the Expanding Your Tutoring Business Series that have also made a positive contribution to the tutoring industry.

This is my first comprehensive book regarding online tutoring; that is, it serves as the blueprint for individuals to start and operate their own quality online tutoring business. I'm a certified teacher, professional tutor, instructional designer, curriculum developer, online professor, educational consultant, and global business owner. I've stepped out on faith to follow my lifelong passion and dream. The information presented in this series is based on insight and actual experiences that I have encountered over the years in building my own global learning organization. I want to share with the world that online tutoring can be effective, but it takes a lot of planning, dedication, and know-how to avoid major pitfalls that come along with implementing a new program.

In this book, you'll find advice on how to position your learning organization to be in demand for online tutoring. My ultimate goal within my professional career and with this book is to inspire and transform others according to their life purpose.

Acknowledgments

I cannot say this enough, but I must give glory to God for helping me realize my potential and purpose in life. Thanks to my editor, Jena Roach, who has helped build confidence in my writing skills and challenged me to expand my ideas.

My Assumptions

In order to provide you with material to meet your unique situation, I had to make some basic assumptions about your tutoring business. I assume the following:

1. You already have started your tutoring practice and want to expand by offering online tutoring services.
2. You have a desire to tutor online and need this information to be successful in operating your online tutoring business.
3. You have working knowledge about tutoring.
4. You have read the other books in the Dr. Alicia Holland's Expanding Your Tutoring Business Series.

Part I:
The Early Stages of Planning Your Online Tutoring Business

CHAPTER 1
Introduction to the Fabulous World of Tutoring

In this chapter, you will:

- Learn why tutoring is in high demand and why parents choose specific tutors.
- Read about the different types of professional tutoring associations.
- Discover the many people who enter the tutoring profession.
- Assess your strengths and weaknesses to help determine your tutoring niche.
- Find your niche and predict your chances for success as a tutor.
- Craft your professional tutor's résumé.

Why Tutoring Is in Demand

"Tutoring is a huge industry in much of Asia and is growing fast elsewhere, particularly in Africa, Europe, and North America," (Bray and Silova, 2006, p. 516). Tutoring is in demand because it's no secret that many children are having problems grasping concepts in class. This can be linked to a variety of factors, including high teacher/

student ratio and peer pressure. In addition, many educators do not have the time or energy to help students after school. Bottom line? Parents are highly concerned about their children's futures and will seek the help that they need in academics.

In today's society, many parents are realizing that they truly have control over their children's education and that many options are available to them to supplement their education. This is where you come into the picture. Oftentimes parents turn to private tutors (or tutoring companies) for assistance.

Another reason that tutoring is in demand is the bipartisan No Child Left behind (NCLB) Act that the United States Congress passed in 2001. The legislation promised high standards, accountability, more choices for parents, and research-based methods of instruction. According to Find a Franchise.com (2010), "When the NCLB Act became the law of the land, the tutoring industry quickly exploded into a staggering four billion dollar business," (para. 4). This opened up new opportunities for people from many walks of life, but it also created the sense that tutors (or tutoring companies) were to be held accountable, along with parents, teachers, administrators, and other key stakeholders in the educational system.

As the tutoring industry was growing exponentially, so did the need for professional tutoring associations. In the next section, we will explore the different types of professional tutoring associations.

Professional Tutoring Associations

In any profession, professional associations are necessary for providing a safe haven for professionals to learn and grow. Well, this type of professionalism did not occur in the tutoring profession until 1990. After 1990, several worthy tutoring associations formed and have gained respect in the tutoring industry. Let's look at the tutoring associations that were formed toward the end of the twentieth century. These associations were the Association of Educators in Private Practice (AEPP) and the National Tutoring Association.

Association of Educators in Private Practice (AEPP)

The first tutoring association, founded in 1990, was named the Association of Educators in Private Practice (AEPP). This organization was renamed the Education Industry Association (EIA) in 2002, because the organization wanted to include the variety of enterprises that were providing market-based services. Now, the EIA has over eight hundred corporate and individual members. Thus, it is considered the leading professional association for private providers of education services, suppliers, and other private organizations who are stakeholders in education (EIA, 2010).

National Tutoring Association (NTA)

Just two years later (1992), the second tutoring association, the National Tutoring Association (NTA), made its debut. According to the NTA, this association was formed for the following purpose: "To establish a membership organization for tutoring professionals" (NTA, 2010). In fact, the National Tutoring Association is the largest professional association dedicated exclusively to tutoring. NTA represents the interests of more than 16,000 tutors in the U.S. and 7 other countries, practicing in all phases of tutoring, program administration, and supplemental student services. Members represent colleges, universities, high schools, middle schools, elementary schools, school districts, literacy programs, community programs, grant supported programs, and NCLB/SES providers. Also, NTA welcomes peer, paraprofessional, professional, volunteer, and private practice tutors (NTA, 2010, para. 3).

This organization has been around for more than two decades and has made many positive contributions to the tutoring profession. On the brink of the twenty-first century and the era of No Child Left behind (NCLB), several other tutoring associations were established. These tutoring associations include the American Tutoring Association, the Association for the Tutoring Profession, and the International Tutoring Association.

The American Tutoring Association and the International Tutoring Association

The third association, the American Tutoring Association (ATA), was formed in 2000. This organization is a 501(c)(3) nonprofit organization dedicated to creating excellence in private tutoring (ATA, 2010). This organization provides tutoring certification and credibility as a private tutor. In 2006, Mark Greenwood formed the fifth tutoring association—the International Tutoring Association (ITA). This organization is intended to be a place for tutors to develop their professional talents and techniques.

Tutors are also encouraged to provide professional tips, exchange stories, and share resources (ITA, 2010). Not only does ITA cater to private tutors, but it also provides quality training to university-level programs.

Association for the Tutoring Profession

The Association for the Tutoring Profession (ATP) had its beginnings in 2003; it became ATP in 2004. This organization is not affiliated with any private sector and promotes scholarly research and professional experiences as a tutor in any tutoring setting (i.e., university, private, center-based, etc.) (ATP, 2010).

Now that you have been exposed to the many tutoring associations, are you wondering which association would best supply your needs as a private tutor? Well, let me share my professional experience and advice with you.

International Tutoring and Teaching Symposium

The International Tutoring and Teaching Symposium (ITTS) was formed back in 2016. This is an annual professional tutoring conference that is designed to serve tutors, educators, academic coaches, mentors, tutor business owners, and the supplemental educational service industry around the world. This conference is associated with iGlobal Educational Services and it promotes scholarly research and professional experiences as tutoring and educational practitioners in any educational setting.

> **Expert's Advice:** The best advice that I can give to you is to make sure that your needs are being met at the professional tutoring association. In other words, if you are a private tutor, then you want to make sure that there are topics that can be applied to your specific situation. Otherwise, it may be best to focus on the specific content area in which you tutor and grow in that area.
>
> In an effort to assist you, please make sure that you answer the following questions prior to joining any professional association, especially in the tutoring industry.
>
> 1. What do you want out of the membership?
> 2. Are you looking for certification as a tutor? Which professional tutoring association offers the most benefits for your current and future needs?
> 3. How will joining this organization support your decision to tutor?
>
> These are the three questions that will guide you in making an appropriate decision about joining a tutoring association.

Types of Tutoring

There are various types of tutoring that can occur with learners. Specifically, there are two types of tutoring that can occur with learners that include both individualized tutoring and group tutoring. Both methods are effective for learners, but individuals really have to assess the learner's needs.

In addition, each method can be delivered either in-person in a physical environment or online in a virtual environment. The delivery method is also determined by the learner. Either method is effective.

Just like any other concept, there are advantages and disadvantages of both types of tutoring. Rather than list them out, let's compare the two types so you can make an informed decision on which method is better for your clients.

Individualized Tutoring Sessions	*Small Group Tutoring Sessions*
✧ Entire set time to interact with the tutor. ✧ One Learner. ✧ Same or Multiple Subjects.	✧ Limited time to interact with the tutor. ✧ 3-5 Learners. ✧ Same or Multiple Subjects.

Tutors will have to determine if they are ready to offer small group tutoring sessions. If learners are doing a great job in individual tutoring sessions, then it may be a great idea to continue conducting individualized tutoring sessions.

The bottom line is that both types of tutoring sessions are beneficial to learners, and tutors should conduct these sessions with the learner's best interest in mind.

Who Can Tutor

According to Merriam-Webster's online dictionary (2009), tutoring is "To teach or guide usually individually in a special subject or for a particular purpose," (para. 3). This definition does not restrict any individuals from tutoring. Thus, any person can tutor as long as he or she has both the knowledge and skills to be successful. Specifically, there are seven groups of people who may consider tutoring at some point in their lives. They are the following: (a) high school seniors; (b) college students; (c) degreed professionals; (d) professionals; (e) stay-at-home parents; (f) former military; and (g) retired individuals. Members of each of these groups bring a special set of skills to the tutoring profession. In my opinion, each group is qualified to tutor.

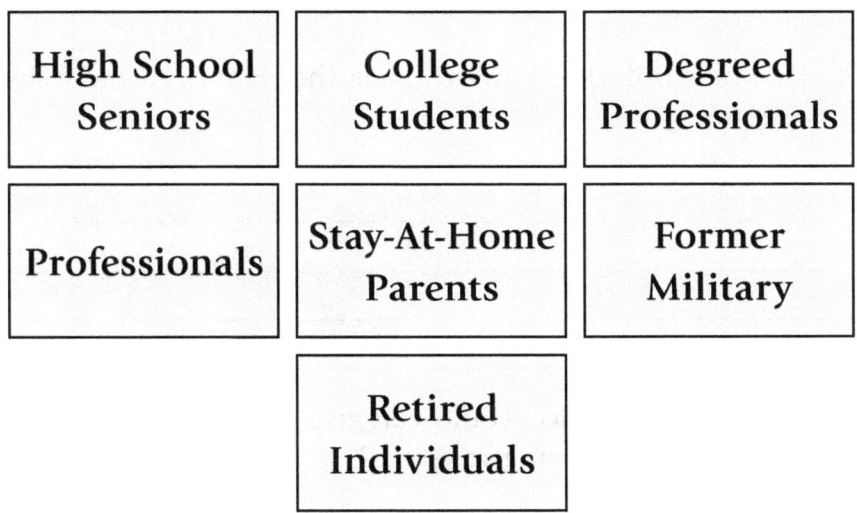

High school seniors are considered adults and are at the legal age where they can offer their services to their friends and/or family members. This allows both college and high school seniors to benefit from referrals and have the opportunity to work as private tutors. Similarly, college students offer their services to the same clientele as high school students, but they have the college experience and credits (at least eighteen hours) in the specific subject area they are tutoring, which is always an added benefit.

••

SCENARIO: *"High School Ambitions"*

Edward, a senior in high school, started helping his friends with calculus and trigonometry. In the summer, he got a tutoring gig at a local community program to work with students who needed help in these topics. Edward was hesitant about taking the gig, but he realized that there were no more offers on the table for a high school student. He could either take the position or be jobless for the summer. Several weeks later, Edward realized that he liked to tutor and would try to help others in the fall, either at the local community center or on his own at a local library.

• •

1. Do you think that Edward made the right decision? Why or why not?

_____
_____
_____
_____
_____

2. What type of advice would you give Edward regarding tutoring since he is starting so young?

_____
_____
_____
_____
_____

Degreed professionals are individuals who hold a bachelor's, master's, or doctorate degree in academia. They typically generalize in a certain area and are considered experts specifically for their program of study. On the other hand, college students are either traditional or nontraditional students working toward a degree; they are typically flexible with their tutoring schedules. Oftentimes these students pick up a range of skills working various jobs and as a result, they are able to relate well to their clients. This group could include substitute teachers as well.

Professionals and stay-at-home parents are people who may or may not hold a degree but have a great deal of experience in a certain subject or area. This qualifies them to tutor others in their specialty areas, such as chemistry, physics, or foreign languages. Stay-at-home parents may opt to offer tutoring services to others for a nominal fee while homeschooling their own children.

Former military and retired individuals may choose to tutor others as a way to stay current with their knowledge while helping others. Members of these two groups make great tutors because of the life experiences they have had and the many different places they have seen throughout their lives. Because tutoring is not a "sit and get" method, these individuals can help clients relate specific content to the real world and apply it to their own lives.

SCENARIO: *"Serving a Higher Purpose"*

Leon, a former navy petty officer, decided to put his leadership and science skills to use. He applied to a local Craigslist posting about tutoring a tenth grader in organic chemistry and got the position. Immediately, he and the tenth grader met at a local coffee shop, which became their permanent spot to meet. Rather than working for a tutoring company, he decided that he would start up his own small tutoring business, given that he already possessed the necessary leadership skills to run a business and be an effective leader. Leon thought to himself, "I am still serving my country one person at a time." Imagine that!

1. Do you know of anyone who followed Leon's footsteps as a tutor? What type of advice would you seek from him or her?

_____

_____

_____

_____

_____

2. What was your reaction to Leon's own self-discovery of his purpose—"I am still serving my country one person at a time"?

Assessing Your Strengths and Weaknesses

Are you considering a tutoring career? Before you can tutor, you need to answer a few questions so you can become aware of what you really want from a tutoring career and what skills you need to do so.

Please write down your answers to the following questions.

1. How much teaching and/or tutoring have you done so far?

2. Which subjects did you teach and/or tutor (be specific— Elementary Math, Algebra I, Spanish II)?

3. What kinds of professional development classes, college courses, or workshops (that specifically focus on tutoring) have you taken? List and give details about each of them.

_____
_____
_____
_____
_____

4. Describe your education. Do you have any degree(s) or advanced degree(s)? Are you a certified teacher?

_____
_____
_____
_____
_____

5. Do you belong to any professional organizations, including professional tutoring organizations? If so, list them.

_____
_____
_____
_____
_____

6. What experience do you have with technology? Do you have a fax machine? Do you have a website or a blog?

_____
_____
_____
_____
_____

7. What do you think are your strengths as a tutor? What are your weaknesses? Explain.

8. How well do you work with others? Explain.

9. How supportive is/are your significant other or family members of your tutoring career? Explain.

10. Do you have any experience in customer service? If so, list your experience.

11. How often do you set personal goals for yourself? Do you achieve these goals? Why or why not?

_____
_____
_____
_____
_____

12. How would you rate yourself, on a scale of one to ten with one being the lowest and ten being the highest, with time management and organization? Why?

_____
_____
_____
_____
_____

13. How much money would you like to eventually make each year from tutoring? How much money do you need to start making right away from your tutoring business? Explain in detail.

_____
_____
_____
_____
_____

Your responses to these questions will help you assess your strengths and weaknesses. Also, they will help you discover the skills you already have to make your tutoring business successful (or the ones you lack).

Finding Your Niche and Predicting Your Chances for Success

If you took time to answer the previous questions, you probably discovered some things about yourself that gave you specific areas to work on in building your tutoring business. Maybe you realized that tutoring requires more dedication than you thought and that you may need to take additional academic classes to hone your tutoring skills and content knowledge.

In the next few weeks (or months), you should develop an action plan to improve these areas, prior to opening your tutoring business. In addition, you should have enough information to create a tutoring résumé.

Crafting Your Professional Tutor's Résumé

A résumé for a professional tutor should be succinct but informative.

Prospective clients want to skim a résumé to find the most important qualities they feel are necessary for a tutor. As with any other résumé, you want to make sure that you include the following sections: (1) education; (2) teaching and/or tutoring certifications; (3) first aid, AED, or CPR certifications; (4) teaching/tutoring experience; (5) skill set; (6) professional organizations; and (7) references.

Here are the reasons these components are important.

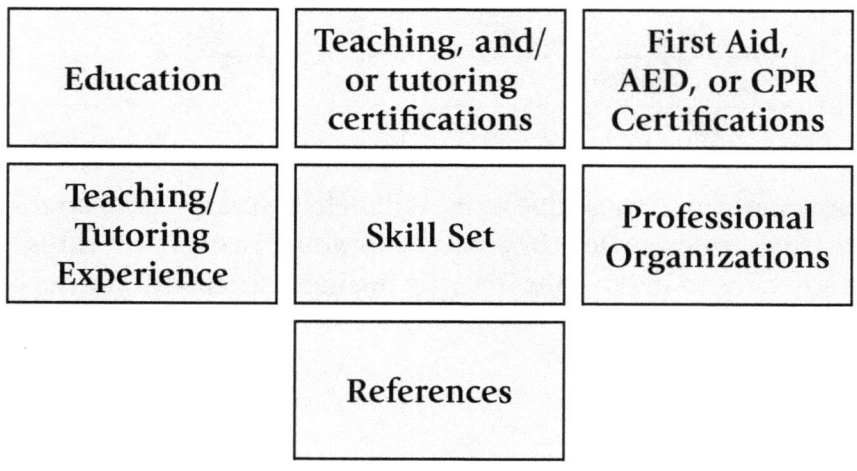

Education

First of all, your educational level lets the prospective clients know that you have the content knowledge and motivation to further your studies. For example, if you are a college student with a certain number of hours in a specific content area, then you would be highly qualified to tutor that specific area based upon your education and practical experience working with that content area.

Teaching and/or Tutoring Certifications

Your certifications also serve as a quick assessment of whether you are qualified in the areas in which prospective clients are seeking your services.

First Aid/AED (Automated External Defibrillator)/ CPR Certification

This certification should be considered with all clients, but especially if you are considering working with clients who have special needs. Some clients will only choose tutors who have this type of certification, so it's definitely worth pursuing.

Teaching/Tutoring Experience

Prospective clients want to know if you have the necessary experience to work with them or their child. Therefore, for both teaching and tutoring experiences, please list out the various types of learners in which you have worked with to showcase that you have experience working with diverse learners.

Skill Set

Your skill set will showcase the qualities that you offer to your clients. This includes characteristics like being positive, flexible, organized, emotionally intelligent, and technology savvy and having strong interpersonal skills. By listing your skill set, you save time in the interview.

Just so that you know, parents will test you to see if these characteristics are present, and if they are (or are not), it will show during the interview or consultation.

Professional Associations

Your involvement in professional associations will show that you are "in the know" about state-of-the-art and research-based methods. Also, it shows that you are a lifelong learner.

References

Your references can be considered the lifeblood of your tutoring business; they can either make or break it. By listing your tutoring references, you will show that you are confident in your services and are valued as a tutor. Please be cautious about putting "Available upon request" on your résumé. This can be seen as having a negative connotation, which means you are too confident (arrogant) or may be hiding something. So, it's important to make sure you have at least three references; they should be three satisfied clients who have received three different services from you (i.e., test prep, math, and reading tutoring).

In this chapter, you learned why tutoring is in high demand and who could enter the tutoring profession. You were also able to assess your own strengths and weaknesses to find your tutoring niche, as well as revamp your résumé as a professional tutor. Are you ready for your own tutoring business? Well, it's time to explore how to start and legalize your tutoring business.

CHAPTER 2
Becoming a Legitimate Online Tutoring Company

In this chapter:
- Creating a vision and mission statement
- Selecting a business name
- Filing for a business structure
- Selecting a logo and corporate identity package
- Assessing start-up needs and budgets

Up to this point, you have probably been doing business under an assumed name, which is fine. Are you ready to take your tutoring business to the next level? Before you can file for a business, you must create a vision and mission statement to help with selecting a business name and other identity for your tutoring business.

Creating a Vision and Mission Statement

You probably already have both a vision and mission statement in mind. If you are already running a home-based tutoring business, then you want to examine these statements to gain inspiration so that you can move your tutoring business forward.

Take a look at three powerful questions to help you create your vision and mission statement.

1. How many target market(s) do you plan to serve? Identify them.

_____
_____
_____
_____
_____

2. What is the purpose of your learning organization?

_____
_____
_____
_____
_____

3. How do you plan to serve your clients?

_____
_____
_____
_____
_____

> **Expert's Advice:** You may already know these answers, or you may need to see the logo before putting your vision on paper. Thus, I think that you should do what fits naturally.

Selecting a Business Name

Your business name will be how people recognize your services and products. In the business world, this is referred to as branding. You want to make your business stand out so others will know that you are unique. As a sole proprietor, you can be extremely creative or simple.

Select a business name that embodies both your vision and mission statement. Make it unique. In other words, choose wisely.

Please write down your answers to the following questions. Your responses will guide you in making the right choice about selecting a business name for your learning organization.

1. What does your business stand for?

_____
_____
_____
_____
_____

2. When potential clients look at your business name, what would you like for them to see? Name at least seven adjectives.

_____
_____
_____
_____

Adjective List:

_____
_____
_____
_____
_____

3. How would your business name define all the services and products?

_____
_____
_____
_____
_____

4. Will your business name survive growth? Why or why not? Will the name of your company transition with future growth?

_____
_____
_____
_____

5. List at least three potential business names, along with taglines, to represent the services and products offered.

_____
_____
_____
_____

6. Ask trusted individuals which business name sounds professional. How did they respond?

_____
_____
_____
_____

7. What is your intuition telling you about your potential business name?

_____
_____
_____
_____

Expert's Advice: Selecting the business name is the most important aspect of building a global learning organization. I know firsthand how selecting the right business name impacts the direction your organization will take.

When I started out locally as a private tutor, I was doing business as Realistic Measures & Consulting. At that time, my private home-based tutoring business was focusing on realistic results according to the student's learning needs. Thus, my tagline was "Believe in Yourself and Go Far"™.

After expanding my tutoring business into a learning organization, the business structure changed. It was the perfect time to reevaluate a new business name. In March 2011, iGlobal Educational Services was born.

iGlobal Educational Services was selected because our vision is to serve a global market, for which we are currently providing. While I still have the personal belief of "Believe in Yourself and Go Far," I kept my organization's new motto under this theme. iGlobal Educational Services' tagline is the following: "Believe. Inspire. Transform."™ It represents the past, present, and future of how my tutoring business has evolved into a great learning organization to help others.

Filing for a Business Structure

There are many business structures available to consider. You must visit your accountant or seek a free consultation to fully understand the options. Most tutoring companies are formed as Limited Liability Companies (LLC). However, there are other choices to choose from, which are outlined on the next page.

Sole Proprietary	Limited Liability Company	Partnership
• Working as an independent contractor.	• Owned by one or more individuals. • Members can function as a corporation. • Working as a company and hiring employees and/or independent contractors.	• Owned by two individuals. • Working as a company and hiring employees and/or independent contractors.

Scenario: "Merry-Go Round"

Destiny Purpose, a well-sought reading tutor in her community, anticipated an additional annual income of $5,000 just from her part-time tutoring. She operated her tutoring business as a sole proprietor and took on the assumed name of "Destiny's Tutoring Services." At the end of the tax year, she tallied all expenses related to her home-based business and quickly realized that she had spent over $1,000 and earned $5,000 in additional income.

For the past two years, she had been doing her own taxes using the online tax software. When she entered the required information, she was shocked to learn that she had to pay money to the Internal Revenue Service (IRS). That very next day, she called a local accountant and scheduled a free consultation. The accountant explained that those numbers were very likely because of her business structure, which was a sole proprietorship. Thus, the accountant recommended that she formed an LLC due to her specific tax information.

This business structure change would open up the door for promptly deducting business expenses and other perks. However, more paperwork is involved such as accounting, payroll and taxes, annual meetings with published minutes, and other required documentation. The accountant did say that a new business name would have to be established. Destiny was devastated because she knew how hard it would be to start over. However, she kept a positive attitude and thanked the accountant.

> **Expert's Advice:** Knowledge is power. It was wise of Destiny to contact this accountant because she was able to learn that she now needed to legalize her business as a corporation, a sub-chapter corporation for LLCs.
>
> From a business perspective, this is incredibly significant. Destiny started out as a sole proprietor to build her clientele and demand for her tutoring services. When it came time to take her business to the next level, she was able to do so. Since this is very new to her, I would recommend that Destiny continue to take steps to educate herself. This will help her build a dynamic learning organization.

Where to Look for Help

After deciding on a business structure and submitting the necessary legal paperwork, it is time to get some additional business insight. Did you know that there are organizations that are willing to help entrepreneurs, like yourself, start a new business?

Here are some places to help you get started:

1. SCORE
2. The Small Business Administration (SBA)
3. Publications [i.e. www.entrepreneur.com and www.becomingabettertutor.com]
4. Local University Small Business Development Center
5. City and State Resources

Selecting a Logo and Corporate Identity Package

This is one of the fun parts of starting a business! You will need to select a logo to set yourself apart from your competition. It is best to get a corporate identity package that includes a logo design, business card, and other design of your choice. However, if you are on a budget, try to get the logo first.

A typical corporate identity package will include the following items:

Typical Corporate Identity Package	
Item	Purpose
Logo Design	Sets your business apart from others. It's your brand name for your services and products.
Letterhead	Identifies communication from the company; this can be created by using only the logo files.
Business Card	Informs potential clients that you're in business. This is an absolute necessity for your tutoring company.
Post Card	Drives traffic to your tutoring business.
Presentation Folder	Shows professionalism with tutoring services.
Brochure Design	Showcases all services and products to potential clients.
Flyer	Drives traffic to your tutoring business.

Each of these marketing materials is very important. However, a priority list can be created based upon your tutoring business's needs.

Expert's Advice: From my own personal experience, I started out with the basic corporate identity package. This included a logo and business-card design. Typically logo designs can be saved in various formats, which results in saving money for a letterhead design.

Another necessity was a website. When I asked clients how they found me, the number one response was always online. Therefore, I made more investments in my website design and utilize other marketing strategies.

Assessing Start-Up Needs and Budget

If you are already in business, then this may be a breeze for you because you got everything that you already need, or so you think.

When starting a corporation, individuals will quickly learn that there are requirements that must be in place before getting an office space in a commercial setting or even taking on state and federal contracts.

Below is a list of items that you will need to budget:

1. Office Supplies
2. Office Space
3. Software
4. Marketing Materials
5. Payroll and Taxes
6. Office Technology
7. Business Insurances
8. Software
9. Outsourcing
10. Travel
11. Professional Development

Let's take a look at the various types of items that will need to be budgeted and why they are important to helping your tutoring business flourish.

Office Supplies Budget

The first item that will need to be budgeted is office supplies. This includes technology, software, and furniture.

Common office supplies that will be used regularly are listed below:

- Presentation folders
- File folders
- Label Maker
- Pens and Pencils

- Clipboard
- Boxes
- Jump drives
- CDs (recordable)
- Highlighters
- White-out
- Permanent markers
- Paper clips
- Color paper
- Envelopes (all sizes)
- Binder clips
- All-purpose copy paper
- Stapler (Heavy duty)

Office Technology

Common office technologies that will be used regularly are listed below:

- Fax machine
- Copier (Laser)
- iPad
- Lots of Ink and Toner
- Computers (Desktop and Laptop)
- Microphone Headset
- Phone Line
- Printer

Software

Common software for the office that will be used regularly is listed below:

- Microsoft Professional Office
- Adobe Creative Suite

- LiveScribe Pen
- My Attorney Software

Office Furniture

Common furniture for the office that will be used regularly is listed below:

- Bookcases
- Chairs and tables
- Conference table
- Receptionist desk
- Office desks
- Trash cans
- Filing cabinets (Secured)

In addition to these, you need to budget for miscellaneous items such as décor. While this budget does not have to be huge, careful consideration should be used when trying to decorate your office to create a positive business environment.

Even if your business is online, you still need to have your office decorated whether it is seasonal or year-round. This puts you in a professional frame of mind to complete your best work. Not to mention, if you do have clients who occasionally meet with you face-to-face, they will see that you are no amateur and conduct business as a professional.

Office Space Budget

The next item that you should budget for is office space. (See Dr. Alicia Holland's *Expanding Your Tutoring Business: The Blueprint to Building a Global Learning Organization* for information on assessing your office space needs).

Whether you desire to work from home or at an alternative location, you will still need a place to do your work free of distractions and wandering eyes. When you are working with intellectual property you must protect it, even at your home.

> **Expert's Advice:**
>
> You may not think about it if you are working out of your home, but you need to save money now. As a sole proprietor, it may be so tempting to take and spend every dollar…and in some cases, you have to cover certain expenses. Thus, the goal is to save 25 percent of each project toward rent.
>
> For instance, let's say that you made $1,000 per month for tutoring services.
>
> From that, 10 percent of $1,000 is $100 while 5 percent of $1,000 is $50. Thus, when that amount is added, we have 25 percent of $1,000 is $250.
>
> Based upon this example, this tutor should be saving $250 if he or she makes $1,000. In other words, individuals should be saving 25 percent of each project toward rent expenses that are occurred monthly.
>
> I highly recommend reading and completing the exercises in Chapter 2 (See Dr. Alicia Holland's *Expanding Your Tutoring Business: The Blueprint to Building a Global Learning Organization*) for information on assessing your office space needs and setting an office space budget. This will provide better insight into your tutoring business's needs and will help you plan appropriately.

Marketing Budget

The third item that you need to budget is marketing materials. While you may have a huge list ready to try to promote your tutoring business, it is best to choose your marketing strategies wisely. In my first tutoring book, *Becoming a Better Tutor: A Data-Driven Approach to Tutoring*, I mention that there are two types of marketing strategies. These include both basic and advanced marketing strategies.

Below is a table of each type of strategies listed under the appropriate marketing category:

Basic Marketing Strategies	Advanced Marketing Strategies
Online Advertising	Offering Sponsorships
Local Advertising	Website
Networking	Direct mailing and Newsletters
	Joining your Local Chamber of Commerce

(Holland-Johnson, 2010, pp. 28-29)

In addition to these listed strategies, individuals should be using more advanced strategies to connect with new and existing clients.

Don't assume that because your business is expanding, you also have to expand your marketing budget. This is not the case, though extra funds are beneficial when applying to those advanced marketing strategies such as press releases.

Payroll and Taxes Budget

The fourth item you will need to budget for is payroll and taxes. It is expected that employers set up an account with the state workforce agency. If you have hired a payroll company to help you with these needs, they will help manage this account when payroll is run each month. The main advantage of working with a payroll company is that they are held responsible. In fact, if there is an error on their behalf, they will pay for it.

Common tax reporting includes the following:

1. **Sales and Use Tax**
2. **Franchise Tax**

These types of taxes can be filed by you. When it comes time to start paying yourself, then you will need to start looking for experienced and trustworthy payroll companies that are cost-effective and exceptional in customer service. When hiring a company to do payroll and taxes, you should look for businesses that can provide full-service payroll and tax filings. It would not hurt to see if it also offers additional human resource services.

> **Expert's Advice:**
>
> You may think that it is not important to do payroll and taxes. This is only true if you are working as a sole proprietor because you get to keep what you make.
>
> As a learning organization, it is very important to begin running payroll and reporting taxes. There are many organizations, including software that can calculate payroll and taxes. Depending on the state in which you are conducting business, there are certain requirements such as sales-tax and franchise-tax reporting.
>
> When it comes to taxes at either the state or federal levels, it is best that you contact these tax agencies on your own. For example, Texas business owners would contact the state comptroller's office regarding any questions related to sales and tax use. When it comes to federal taxes, the best point of contact is the Internal Revenue Service (IRS).
>
> Whether you decide to sell products or not, you are still required to apply for sales permit that lists your place of business.
>
> When I expanded my tutoring business, all these taxes were very new to me. I quickly learned that I had made the best decision to start out as a home-based tutoring business. I searched online for local business courses for small business owners and was very blessed to find a workshop related to taxes. I was proud to pay $35 to attend this workshop because it helped me start out on the right road with business tax obligations.

Business Insurance Budget

The fifth item is to seek business insurance. If you get your own lease agreement, you will need business insurance prior to moving into the office space. Depending on your organizational structure, you will need (at minimum) the following types of business insurances.

1. **Professional Liability**

This type of insurance protects professional advice and service companies from negligence claims. For example, if you find yourself in a situation that may involve damages or other issues, then this will cover you and your business.

2. **Automobile Insurance**

If your business has vehicles that are used by tutors or to transport students, it is required to have this type of insurance. If your business does not have any vehicles for business use, then it is in your best interest to provide a written explanation when submitting bids to complete various projects. This is only if the project requires showing proof of business insurances and coverage.

3. **Worker's Compensation Liability Insurance**

This is another type of insurance that is needed to be in business. It covers any accidents on the job. Most state and federal contracts require worker's compensation liability insurance.

Outsourcing Budget

The sixth item that needs to be budgeted is outsourcing projects. There will be some projects that you will not have time to do or know how to do. Therefore, it is very important to pay an expert to complete them. For example, these projects can range from accounting writing, lead generation, and so forth.

> **Expert's Advice:** Don't enter into outsourcing thinking that you do not have to check on the contractor. In reality, you will have to lead them in order to get the desired outcome. Otherwise, you will become bitter and disappointed. You must understand what you want and provide written instructions.

Travel Budget

The seventh item is a travel budget. You will need to budget for travel, even if you work online. It is expected that you will attend professional development opportunities such as conferences or other informative opportunities. You may also need to budget for business trips that may be outside of your geographical area. Items that should be budgeted are the following:

Gas

Hotel

Meals

Toll fees

Air fare and associated fees

Bus fare

Taxi fare

Rentals

Professional Development Budget

The last item is professional development. Let's face it; no one knows everything. That's why we take courses to further our knowledge base. Specifically, in your tutoring business, there will be many things that you will need to learn to stay competitive in such a global economy.

Below are some recommended business courses to help you be successful with your tutoring business:

1. QuickBooks
2. Intellectual Property
3. Tax Requirement
4. Record-Keeping
5. Leadership
6. Customer Service
7. Social Media Marketing

While many conferences are offered throughout the year, it is very important to carefully select which ones you will attend. Traveling to conferences can be costly, but you get to see some very exciting places and meet different people from many walks of life.

You have been presented with good information that can help you begin to think about how you want to birth your learning organization. Proper planning and assessment of your tutoring business needs will lead you to a greater chance of success with your organization.

Part II:
Establishing and Promoting Your Online Tutoring Business

CHAPTER 3
Selecting an Online Tutoring Platform

You may be ready to start your e-learning or online tutoring program, but there are several tasks that must be considered. These tasks include the following: (a) Finding a suitable online tutoring platform; (b) Creating a process that will make your online tutoring business run smoothly; (c) Creating a plan for conducting online tutoring sessions and data-reporting; and (d) Addressing how to communicate within the virtual classroom. Each of these tasks will be discussed along the way as you read each chapter in this book.

Guidelines for Selecting an Online Tutoring Platform

When it comes time to selecting an online tutoring platform, you need to be aware of the many platforms available. In addition, you need to make sure that you are catering to your clients' needs, not just your budget. With this perspective, you can be better prepared before you make your selection. To help with this process, there are some questions that will guide you into making a well-informed decision. Let's look at these questions on the next page.

1. How will you record attendance to verify that learners came to sessions?

2. Will the virtual classroom accommodate all learning modalities? Why or why not?

3. What is the pricing for the virtual platform? Does it include annual licensing fees?

4. Will the virtual classroom accommodate all learning modalities? Why or why not?

5. What is the pricing for the virtual platform? Does it include annual licensing fees?

___

6. How will clients log-on to the system? Is there a sign-in page or will you send them session links?

___

7. What are your administrative tasks, and how will they impact you conducting online tutoring sessions?

___

> **Expert's Advice:** These are some questions to get you thinking about your online tutoring program. I want to share with you my top capabilities in a virtual classroom. This will be very important if you plan on working with other organizations to provide online tutoring services. You have to understand that online tutoring is still relatively new. As a result, you must be able to deliver so that your business will soar and your efforts will help promote online tutoring in a positive fashion.

Expert's Advice: *(continued)*

Here's what your online tutoring business should have for its e-learning program and my rationale behind it:

1. Chat Feature
   a. *Benefit for Students*: The chat feature is used primarily for interacting with class, if more learners are present. If not, then this is an individual way of asking questions for the tutor.
   b. *Benefit for Tutors:* Tutors are able to pose questions, write directions, or view problems in the chat feature. This comes in handy so that students can actually see the problem. Also, you need to check to see if there is a copy-and-paste feature so that it saves them.
   c. *Learning Styles Addressed:* kinesthetic, tactile, and visual.
2. Whiteboard (With Multiple Boards)
   a. *Benefit for Students*: The learners are able to use their visual learning style. They are able to write on the whiteboard, which makes it an interactive lesson. For example, if students need to explain their thinking, then they can draw it on the whiteboard.
   b. *Benefit for Tutors:* Tutors are able to reference more than one whiteboard at a time. Tutors have the ability to restrict learner access on the whiteboard, if deemed necessary. Tutors are able to deliver instruction, just as they were in a traditional classroom that either had a whiteboard or interactive whiteboard.
   c. *Learning Styles Addressed:* kinesthetic, tactile, and visual.
3. Webcam
   a. *Benefits*: There should be a webcam feature available so that you can see the learner and he or she can see you. This will take the guesswork out of whether you are tutoring that learner or not. You can actually see him or her and he or she can see you.

Expert's Advice: *(continued)*

Please note that you will only be able to see their face and surrounding area where the camera is displayed. Depending on whether you are using a laptop or desktop, it will determine if your clients are able to see you. This will be an added benefit to your online tutoring program. It will definitely add credibility that real tutors are being used in online tutoring sessions.

b. *Learning Styles Addressed:* visual

4. Media

a. *Benefits:* A virtual classroom should have the capability of playing media in the classroom. Often times, tutors will enhance their lessons by providing two- to three-minute (no more than five minutes) video clips to show how the concepts are tied to the real world and so forth. In addition to the chat and interactive whiteboard feature, this feature makes the learning environment more conducive to engaging and interesting tutoring sessions.

b. *Learning Styles Addressed:* visual

5. Recording Feature

a. *Benefits:* You want to make sure that all interaction in the classroom can be recorded for multiple purposes.

The first purpose is to provide documentation that actual tutoring sessions are being conducted and authorized individuals can view the session recordings to verify this information.

The second purpose is to improve the quality of tutoring sessions, while the third purpose is to evaluate tutor performance and allow tutors to self-evaluate their tutoring sessions.

b. *Learning Styles Addressed:* visual

Expert's Advice: *(continued)*

6. *Capability to View and Send a Variety of Files*

    a. *Benefit for Students*: Just like the traditional setting, both tutors and learners will be expected to view and send a variety of files. For example, students may need assistance with a certain set of problems, which will have to be uploaded to the tutor.

    b. *Benefit for Tutors:* Tutors want to also be able to view documents on the whiteboard so that learners are able to view a presentation or work a few problems together.

    c. *Learning Styles Addressed:* kinesthetic, tactile, and visual.

7. *Automated Attendance Report*

    a. *Benefits*: You need to make sure the virtual classroom has an attendance feature that captures both the tutor and participant time spent in the classroom. It also needs to capture the overall time spent in the tutoring session and the names of all participants involved in the tutoring session.

    When you are shopping for a virtual classroom platform, these are the requirements that should be critical to your e-learning program. Most importantly, it will help you have the foundation necessary to deliver top-notch instruction to your clients.

    b. *Learning Styles Addressed:* visual

8. *Group Participant Features*

    a. *Benefits*: You may not be offering group-tutoring sessions at the moment, but you should purchase a virtual classroom platform that has the capability to plan for future organizational needs. There are virtual classrooms that can hold up to at least 10 or more participants at one time.

Expert's Advice: *(continued)*

This feature can also be used to host your organizational trainings and monthly meetings. This depends on how your tutoring business is structured and how your business is run. In my professional opinion, you want to save as much money as possible where you can without jeopardizing payroll or other important organizational needs. If you research online, you will discover that the costs are very expensive and may not make sense if you are a small tutoring company. Therefore, it would be in your best interest to select an online tutoring platform that can also be used for training purposes.

   b. *Learning Styles Addressed:* kinesthetic, tactile, and visual.

9. *Sign-In/Log-In Features*

   a. *Benefits*: Ideally, this is where you want to have your clients log-in from your own website. Depending on your finances, you may want to make an initial investment by starting small rather than shelling out a lot of loot that will be used for other purposes to run your tutoring business.

   There are virtual classrooms that have session links that can be emailed to tutors and clients. Just a heads up, this is a lot of work, but you can learn a lot about how your virtual classroom interface works. This will strictly depend on your budget for this aspect of your tutoring business.

   b. *Learning Styles Addressed:* kinesthetic, tactile, and visual.

Scenario: "Let's Have a Chat Only Class"

Desmond, a Supplemental Educational Services (SES) Provider, decides that he will apply to become a SES provider in another state, besides the one in which he resides. His proposed tutoring program only has the chat feature and a whiteboard. His tutors do not speak English, but they are very knowledgeable in the subject area and are highly educated. His organization has been successful globally and has a track record of helping students that cater to visual learning.

1. How could Desmond improve his tutoring program for *all* students?

2. From an organizational standpoint, what type of training is required for chat-only tutors? Are there training scripts for tutors in their home language? How is this handled?

3. From a parental perspective, would you want your child to receive tutoring from this provider? Why or why not? How does your child like to learn?

Scenario: "A Heaven-Sent Deal...Really?"

Jaimaica Johnson serves her community by offering both math and reading tutoring. She was recently offered a state contract under the federal No Child Left Behind (NCLB) Act and really had to look for an online tutoring platform. Not to mention, she did not have any tutors on board so she panicked.

One beautiful day, she checked her email and found an email from a company who offered both an online tutoring platform and their tutors. Can you imagine how Jaimaica felt? Initially, she was very excited about the offer until she found out the details and saw the contract. In a nutshell, Jaimaica figured that she would pay an annual license fee for $1,000 plus a monthly fee based upon the number of students served. Not to mention, the contract stated that she had to pay the monthly fee whether students were present or not. Last but not least, she was still responsible for paying the tutors, but could not train or communicate with them. After several days of thinking about this deal and realizing in the contract that these tutors could not offer Reading/English Language Arts (ELA) tutoring, Jaimaica quickly turned down the offer and opted to do it herself.

1. Do you think that Jaimaica made the right decision? Why or why not?

2. From an organizational standpoint, what type of business sense did this make, if any?

3. What are your recommendations to Jaimaica?

Scenario: *"Designing on a Quarter"*

Justin Davis had searched around, but had not found the virtual classroom platform that met his organizational needs and was cost-effective for an emerging tutor business. Disgusted with his options, Justin decided that he would fund the design of his own virtual classroom. When he started talking to developers, he was quoted at least $15K to build requirements that met 95 percent of his organizational needs. Justin had to make the decision to continue face-to-face tutoring sessions until he could afford the online tutoring platform.

1. Do you think that Justin should give up or wait? Why or why not?

_____
_____
_____
_____
_____

2. How could have Justin benefitted from finding a cost-effective online tutoring program?

_____
_____
_____
_____
_____

3. Do you think that it is worthwhile to create a proprietary online tutoring platform in a market that is saturated? Why or why not?

_____
_____
_____
_____
_____

CHAPTER 4
Organizational Needs for Your Online Tutoring Business

When you are operating an online tutoring business, it takes a lot of preparation. It is totally different than running an on-ground learning organization. In this chapter, I take you through finding clients, managing and working clients, and how to be successful with your tutoring business from an organizational perspective.

Finding New Clients

Let's look at how to bring clients to your tutoring business. It's important to start thinking about the following questions:

1. How will I market my tutoring business?

2. Will I need a website or how can I improve my current website?

3. Who are my potential clients?

Have you answered these questions? If not, it's okay, because we will take a look at the many ways to advertise your tutoring business. If you have answered all these questions and are already tutoring, then maybe it's time to look at other avenues of attracting customers to your business. Let's look at two categories of marketing your services in the tutoring industry—basic marketing strategies and advanced marketing strategies.

Basic Marketing Strategies

Basic marketing strategies are strategies that have low costs and are easy to use when first starting your tutoring business. Oftentimes you are using these strategies and may not even know it. We will explore a few of the marketing strategies that can be used to attract clients to you. These strategies are the following: (1) online advertising, (2) local advertising, and (3) networking.

Online Advertising

Many jobs are being posted online, especially on job search websites, such as Yahoo Jobs. In today's society, there are many tutoring sites where you can post your tutoring profile for a nominal fee. I have used social networking sites, such as Facebook, Twitter, and LinkedIn, as avenues for advertising my services. I also use Craigslist to advertise my services, as Craigslist allows one to post services in numerous categories. In other words, there will only be one copy of the posting visible. Otherwise, Craigslist monitors postings, and if they see that there is a similar or repeated posting, then they will delete the message or flag it as spam. Please use your own judgment when posting and applying for tutoring jobs, as there seem to be scams targeted at tutors. A good rule of thumb is to post only in your area "that›s if you conduct your tutoring sessions in your own home or at your client›s home" and respond to potential clients who are within your geographic region.

Local Advertising

If you prefer to post locally, then you should seek locations where there's a great deal of traffic. While posting flyers in schools may be a great idea, many public school districts do not allow advertisements about tutoring. Others have a rigid, tedious process where one may have to wait several months before gaining exposure. For this reason, I recommend posting services in areas where you are allowed. You could even consider offering your current client an incentive to refer others to your tutoring services.

After clients have made a decision to choose my tutoring services, I offer them a referral coupon so that they can refer others to my tutoring business. In exchange, clients are able to get a free or discounted tutoring session. Word of mouth is the best way to advertise, since potential clients are already aware of how you conduct business as a tutor and have testimonies about their child›s successes. If you show gratification to your satisfied clients, your business will continue to grow.

Networking

Networking is important in every industry. If you are tutoring locally, then it would make sense to partner or serve as a vendor at a local event to market your services. Oftentimes other small businesses will allow you to advertise in their buildings in exchange for the same exposure and/or services. For example, there was a small business owner who owned a salon and whose daughter needed assistance in math, and we informally discussed tutoring in general while I got my hair done. The following day, we held a tutoring consultation and entered into an agreement that for each six sessions she would give me one free hairstyle. This hairstyle ranged from $180.00 upward. After the tutoring consultation, I realized that her daughter only needed six sessions to improve her area of weakness. In this case, both parties were happy. The stylist was able to get the help for her daughter, and I was happy to help her daughter. From a business perspective, each owner demonstrated honesty and commitment and was results-oriented, which resulted in numerous referrals.

Please beware that every client will not be willing to enter such an agreement and tutors should be selective. In any event, networking is a strategy that should be considered, especially if you are a small business owner.

Advanced Marketing Strategies

Advanced marketing strategies are strategies that are used when a business is established and is lucrative enought to attract more clients. We will explore a few of the marketing strategies that can be used to expand your marketing repertoire.

These strategies are the following: (1) offering sponsorships, (2) getting a website started, (3) using direct mailing and newsletters, and (4) joining your local Chamber of Commerce.

Offering Sponsorships

Are you into sports? Local youth sport coaches are always looking for business owners or individuals to sponsor them. This includes providing certain things for them, like buying their uniforms and equipment. This type of sponsorship will allow you visibility with your targeted audience if you plan on working with K-12 students.

Another way to advertise your tutoring business is to sponsor other community events, such as a luncheon for an event. Let's say that you belong to a professional organization; you can always sponsor a lunch or set up a booth that displays your tutoring services. You never know who's from your geographical area.

Getting a Website Started

A website will be a good investment because clients are always surfing the Internet and could easily find your services. There are many web-hosting services available to choose from, such as godaddy.com, yahoo.com, google.com, and others.

When creating your website, please include the following: (1) a home page with an advertisement about your services, (2) services that you offer, (3) information about the company, and (4) contact page for potential clients.

Home Page

Your home page should consist of your advertisement and should entice prospective clients to want to know more about your services. It wouldn't hurt to add a picture or a logo that brands your tutoring business. This is the first place that potential clients will stop, and it should accurately reflect your tutoring business.

Services Page

This is where you should explain why clients should choose you as a private tutor. After that you should list the services that you provide, along with any pricing information. For example, my potential clients must e-mail or call for current rates. This allows you to interact directly with them, enabling you to justify your rates. You may also want to include a column titled, "What's New at [Your Tutoring Business]." In this section you should include any events that have recently occurred or any upcoming events.

About [Your Tutoring Business]'s Page

This is where you provide the history of your tutoring business and how it got started. Most people are interested in how this service becomes available to others. This would also be a great place to post client testimonials to confirm that you do offer high-quality services to your clients.

Contact Us

On your contact page, it's important to have the phone number, address, and e-mail address of your business. Also, if your web servicer has the capability, it would be helpful to have a link for clients to find driving directions to your tutoring business.

In addition, it would be a great idea to include a customer contact form, which allows potential clients to ask questions about your tutoring services and leave their contact information. This allows you to contact them and answer any questions that they may have about your tutoring services.

Using Direct Mailing and Promotional Products

Direct mailing is a marketing strategy worth trying once your business has grown. You can either choose to mail out your marketing materials or use online direct marketing services. In either case, you would need to create a contact list or purchase a contact list of potential clients who may be interested in your tutoring services.

There are various companies you can use to purchase contact information, such as geoselector.com. Promotional products are definitely a great way to give your tutoring business a jump start. These items could be small, such as mouse pads, pens, pencils, notepads, key chains, and other inexpensive items. Ideally, these items would be given out to first-time clients or prospective clients.

Joining Your Local Chamber of Commerce

Does the area where you are locating your tutoring business have a Chamber of Commerce? If so, you should strongly consider joining it once you have found an office space. The investment that you make with the Chamber of Commerce will definitely go a long way for your business. This organization is dedicated to helping new businesses flourish and will provide a network of resources to help build your tutoring business.

It really does not matter which marketing method you use; you should use the strategies that yield the most traffic yet are cost-efficient to your tutoring business. The bottom line is that you stay within your marketing budget while letting your potential clients know that you offer a variety of services that are tailored to them.

Working with New and Returning Clients

You have been marketing for some time now and have found a couple of clients. Are you wondering what should come next for these clients? It's clear that tutoring should occur, but there really is more involved. There's actually a 13-step process that you need to follow. Don't worry...I won't present them all at once, but I will show you a diagram to at least give you an idea before diving into the details for each step.

13-Step Process for Working with New and Returning Clients

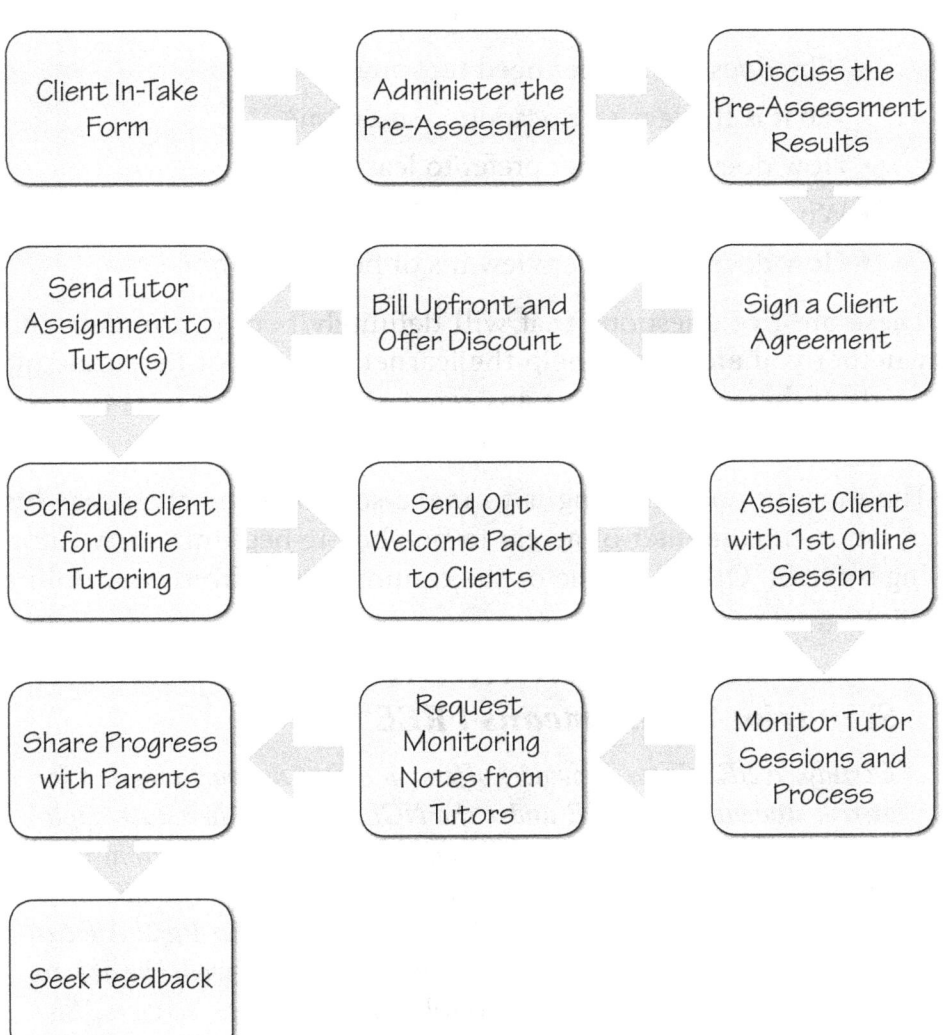

Step 1: Fill the Client In-Take Form

You may be eager to take on this client, but you really need to assess whether you can help him or her. You will do this by scheduling an online tutor consultation or phone consultation. More than likely, you have the basic information in which you need when he or she first inquired. If clients do not have access to the Internet, you may want to complete this information as well.

Here's what you need to know regarding the client intake form:

- Why does the learner need tutoring?
- What is the learner's academic situation?
- How does the learner prefer to learn?
- What is the learner's academic history?
- How does the learner view his or her education?

These are five questions that will definitely help you understand whether you are able to help the learner with his or her academic needs. If these questions are answered, then it will be time to move on to the next step in the 13-step process.

The most important thing is to make sure that the client has his or her own computer or access to one before beginning any tutoring services. Otherwise, he or she cannot benefit from your online tutoring services.

Scenario: "FREE means FREE"

Destiny, a SES Tutor Provider, offers an online tutoring program for at-risk students for FREE under the NCLB Act. In her state application, she listed that students would need to have access from their own computers. However, scholarships were available for families who may need a computer for their child. Given that the Per Pupil Allocation (PPA) is on average $1,000, she thought that she would be able to recoup the cost after providing several hours of tutoring services. She never tells the clients that they will keep the computer, but it is very likely because they may not return it.

Destiny finally got her chance to provide a scholarship to a family in need. The intake process went smoothly and computers and mobile Internet devices were shipped to the student. Several days later, Destiny called to begin online tutoring services and was very surprised. The family did not answer her calls, but confirmed that they did receive the technology on a voicemail message left on her office phone. Destiny was very upset, but she chalked it up as experience and moved on. However, at the next board meeting, the policy of providing scholarship to families was amended where no technology would be offered to clients.

••

1. Do you think that Destiny did the right thing in this situation? Why or why not?

2. From an organizational perspective, how would you have handled this situation?

3. From a parental perspective, how would you feel about a tutoring company who provided your child with both FREE tutoring and learning tools?

> **Expert's Advice:** First of all, it is very unfortunate that the parents missed the opportunity to help their child with their learning needs. Secondly, it is such a shame that Destiny lost revenue due to an unfortunate situation. The reality is that Destiny is in business and must understand that she has to do what is best in the interest of her business. Let me be very clear—Destiny showed compassion and good faith of providing learning tools for the family. In this particular situation, she was looking out for the best interest of students. However, it was the parent who took the ball and ran with it, so to speak. In other words, the parents did their own child injustice, not Destiny.
>
> These are situations in which the state should investigate because it is very unfair to SES providers, such as Destiny. If the client intake process goes smoothly, then it is time to proceed to Step 2, which is to administer the pre-assessments.

Step 2: Administer the Pre-Assessment

In Step 2, this is where you would need to administer the pre-assessment. Depending on how you run your learning organization, you may opt to have students come to the office or take their pre-assessment online. Whatever the method, a pre-assessment should be on file to assess the impact of the tutoring program.

If you are administering an online pre-assessment, you will need to provide directions to help them access the online pre-assessment. Below are sample directions to provide to your clients:

Directions for taking Your Online Pre-Assessment

1. Click on the following web link:
www.linkforonlinepreassessmentgoeshere.com

2. Locate Student Login and Click It.
3. Once you have Clicked On it, you will see a screen that has "Student Login."
4. Please type in your assigned login and password. This will help identify you as the person who is taking this assessment.
5. Your assigned username and password are listed below:
   Username: HollandJohnson3
   Password: 593test
6. Click "Login" to begin the test.

What Happens After I Complete My Test?

It will tell you that you are finished with your test.

How do these test results help me?

These test results help us build lessons for you and measure your progress throughout your online tutoring program. Thus, it is very important for you to take these tests seriously and do your personal best.

If you have any questions or technical support, please contact [insert contact name] at [Insert Phone Number]. You can also reach me directly at [insert phone number] or via email at [youremailaddress@gmail.com].

Good Luck on your test!
[Your Tutoring Business Name]

Step 3: Discuss the Pre-Assessment Results

After the pre-assessment has been taken, it is only natural to discuss the results with the parent. This is the opportunity to seek feedback from the parent and student. It is best to perform these interviews separately because the learner may not always open up while the parent is present.

Below are some sample questions to ask both parents and the learner:

Parent Questions:

1. Are there any other concepts that should be addressed that were not evident in the pre-assessment results? If so, what are they?
2. Do you have any further questions or concerns?

Learner Questions:

1. How do you think that you did on your pre-assessment?
2. Are there specific concepts we need to work on?
3. How do you want us to help you?

These are some questions that can help you with the intake process.

> **Expert's Advice:** The good thing about online pre-assessments is that the results are immediate and depending on the software used for these assessments, detailed reports are available for both parents and tutor business owners.
>
> Once pre-assessment results have been discussed, this is the appropriate time to schedule the client and seek deposits. If this is a client from a federal contract, then you will not need to do this. Once services begin, you can bill the school district.
>
> If you are working with private clients, you should charge for pre-assessments.

Step 4: Sign a Client Agreement Regarding Sessions

At this point in the process, it is deemed necessary to have the client sign a client agreement before doing a lot of administrative work that goes along with new clients. Below are some questions to help you build your own client agreement regarding online tutoring sessions. They are the following:

1. What is your policy regarding assessments? Are clients responsible for payment? Why or why not?

_____
_____
_____
_____
_____

2. What are the tutoring fees?

_____
_____
_____
_____
_____

3. What are the methods of payment? How do you feel about accepting checks?

_____
_____
_____
_____
_____

4. How would you describe the recommended tutoring program?

_____
_____
_____
_____
_____

5. What is the policy for attending online tutoring sessions?

6. How are cancellations handled?

7. What is the policy for "no shows" for both tutors and clients?

8. What are the available tutoring times?

9. What is the policy regarding severe weather and emergencies?

10. What is the scope of the agreement?

11. What is the policy regarding divulging personal information?

12. What is the policy for violating the client agreement?

13. How will clients return the form and sign it? Will it be electronically or via fax?

These are some questions to help you get started with building your very own client agreement.

These next few steps will be done all at once, but want to address each of them separately.

Step 5: Bill Upfront and Offer a Discount

By this time, clients are serious. You need to collect the funds or a non-refundable deposit. Often times, clients may not be able to provide the entire balance so you may want to offer a payment plan, such as 50 percent before the first session, and the other 50 percent before the third session. This method works best when offering tutoring packages. In any event, you should be using invoices with your clients, in programs such as QuickBooks.

> **Expert's Advice:** I highly recommend reading my other books and taking my online tutoring course: Tutor 104: Marketing Your Tutoring Business. These resources will provide you the support necessary with pricing strategies.

Step 6: Send Tutor Assignment to Tutor(s)

Rather than putting the cart before the horse, once Steps 4 and 5 have been completed, this is the appropriate time to seek a qualified tutor in the respective tutoring area. Below are some questions to think about when making tutoring assignments:

1. What is the tutor's availability?

_____
_____
_____
_____

2. What is the tutor's subject area?

_____
_____
_____
_____
_____

3. What did the tutor's performance results?

_____
_____
_____
_____
_____

4. How will this tutor impact the client? Will it be a good fit? Why or why not?

_____
_____
_____
_____
_____

5. What is the tutor's assignment completion rate?

_____
_____
_____
_____
_____

These five questions will aid in placing the best tutors in tutoring assignments that will be a win/win for all. Let's look at a sample tutoring assignment that can be sent via email to a tutor.

Good Afternoon, [Insert Tutor's Name],

Happy Friday! We have an online math tutoring assignment available. It is the following:

9th Grade

Currently, we are waiting to hear back from the school district. It will take anywhere from 1-7 business days for the school district to approve the Student Learning Plan (SLP).

This student has 24 hours and 23 minutes of tutoring hours.

The parent has requested the following tutoring schedule:

Mondays   4:00-5:30PM CST
Tuesdays 4:00-5:30PM CST
Thursdays 4:00-5:30PM CST

Please reply back by Monday, June 18, 2012 (5pm CST) close of business indicating whether you accept or decline this tutoring assignment.

Looking forward to your response,
[Insert Your Name or Tutor Director's Name]

Step 7: Schedule Client for Online Tutoring

Let's be clear; this is about your client. However, it is very important to let clients know when tutors are available. In reality, there cannot be one without the other. In light of this, you need to have the tutor's availability handy as the client is providing his or her schedule. This will increase your chances of getting the client scheduled.

Let's look at two different scenarios to help you understand the importance of having a process in order.

•••

Scenario: "If they can, So can I"

Shelly, a science tutor, took on a tutoring assignment and both parties were content. About 2/3 of the tutoring program, the client missed two sessions and the tutor was paid according to the company's compensa-

tion policy. Without advanced warning, the tutor did not show up to the next scheduled tutoring session. Luckily, the tutor business owner also tutored in that subject area. Therefore, he took over the assignment. As for Shelley, she was coached and a "no show" was recorded in her performance record.

1. How would you have handled this situation, if you were the tutor business owner?

_____
_____
_____
_____
_____

2. Do you think Shelley had that right? Why or why not?

_____
_____
_____
_____
_____

Scenario: "Tutoring or Work—Which One?"

Danielle, a working mom, signed her children up for tutoring when she realized that they had an opportunity to receive free tutoring. Initially, she was very excited about the opportunity and her two girls attended the sessions faithfully...until her mom got a new job.

Rather than let the tutoring company know, Danielle stopped her children from attending because the tutoring times did not work for her. She decided that a later time would have to work. The tutoring company was able to accommodate the family and the two girls finished their 9-week tutoring program.

1. Do you think this was a reasonable accommodation? Why or why not?

2. How would you have handled this situation?

3. How could this been avoided? Was it possible? Why or why not?

Expert's Advice: In Scenario 2: "Tutoring or Work—Which One?", this could not be avoided. The best advice is to work with the parent because she is already under stress. If it turns out that the learner will have a great deal of time pass until the next tutoring session, then it is best to explain to the parent why you cannot work with their child again. The bottom line is that tutoring should not be viewed as an added burden to the client or tutor.

Step 8: Send Out Welcome Packets to Clients

Most of your clients may have their first tutoring experience with you. Therefore, you need to have a welcome packet for your clients (and new tutors, too). Specifically, our focus is on online tutoring businesses and we need to look at welcome packets according to this mode of instruction. Let's look at the components of a welcome packet for new online clients:

a. Welcome Letter from the President
b. Sales Copy and Business Card
c. Hours of Operation/Scheduled Holidays
d. What to Expect
e. Program Survey
f. White Paper—Condensed Form
g. Session and Recording Links or Login Information
h. Contact/Tech Support Information
i. Late Session Policy/Tutor Agreement
j. Tutoring Schedule/Instructional Plan
k. Complimentary e-book
l. Promotional product
m. Monthly Newsletters
n. Access to Your Blog

A. Welcome Letter

This sends a nice, warm welcome that can make another good impression for your company.

> **Expert's Advice:** You really have to understand that you are working with families and should be building a relationship rather than looking at each tutoring agreement. The reality is that you are running a business, but always remember that PEOPLE come first. If you approach your business in this manner, you will make a significant difference in the lives of your clients.

B. Sales Copy and Business Cards

This is the appropriate time to include your marketing material, which could be a brochure or one-sheet page regarding your tutoring services. In addition to this sales copy, you should also include a business card. It is best practice to include at least two business cards. This can be a great way to get your tutoring business noticed and out into the community. It is also a good idea to ask them to share your business card with a friend.

C. Hours of Operation/Scheduled Holidays

If you have not told your clients, then you will need to let them know about the hours of operation and any scheduled holidays.

Below are some typical hours of operation and scheduled holiday closings:

Hours of Operations
Monday thru Friday	12-8pm CST
Saturday	10-2pm CST
Sunday	4-8pm CST

Scheduled Holidays

Spring Break	Summer Break
Fall Break	Winter Break
President's Day	Valentine's Day
Martin Luther King Jr. Day	Memorial Day

These are some examples that can be used to help you plan your hours of operations and scheduled holidays.

D. *What to Expect*

This is your opportunity to explain to client what they can expect. Often times, when you speak with them again, they may not have the exact details. Therefore, this is just another added benefit for your clients. Here are some questions to help draft a one-page checklist of what can be expected:

1. What can clients expect regarding tutoring services?
2. How often will progress be reported?
3. What days and times are available for online tutoring services?
4. What are the tutor qualifications for the specific tutor assigned to clients?
5. How will you communicate to clients and what is the timeframe in which you will do so?

E. *Program Survey*

You may place a copy of the program survey or at least mention it to clients so that they are aware of customer feedback. You may also opt to later email it to clients who have provided an email address close to the end of their online tutoring program.

F. *White Paper (Condensed)*

This is an opportunity to educate your clients about the education industry, specifically regarding tutoring.

G. Session Links/Log-In Information

You will need to provide the log-in information and/or session links so that clients can log in to the virtual classroom successfully.

H. Contact/Tech Support Information

There will be technological glitches as is expected with technology. However, you should provide the contact information so that clients know how to reach the office.

I. Client Agreement

A copy of the client agreement should be included for easy access, along with company policy regarding tutoring services.

J. Tutoring Schedule with Student Learning Plan (SLP)

A copy of the SLP should be included so that clients will know what needs to be covered throughout the online tutoring program. In addition, it is very important to include the tutoring schedule.

K. Complimentary Book or e-book

Clients would appreciate a free resource to help their children at home. When you are providing resources, the focus should be on your clients, not trying to sell your company.

L. Promotional Products

It is a great idea to provide your client with a meaningful promo product that can get your tutoring business exposure, as well as, help them. This is another small token that will set your tutoring business apart.

M. Monthly Newsletters

A copy of the most recent monthly newsletters for clients should be included as well.

N. Information about your Company's Blog

Another great way to connect with clients is to provide a blog that can help them with their children. Visit www.parentseducatechildren.blogspot.com to see an example of how a blog might work for your tutoring business.

These are some components or items that should be included in your tutor company's Welcome Packet for new clients.

Step 9: Assist Client with First Online Tutoring Session

Just like any other new concept, support is needed. You may decide that you want to send out written instructions, but you will still need to follow-up with a phone call. This call should be made at least 30 minutes before the scheduled tutoring session.

Please know that you may need to help the client more than once to ensure that they are successful with logging into the course.

Step 10: Monitor Tutoring Sessions and Progress

Clients and tutors should be made aware that all online tutoring sessions are recorded and will be monitored. This is very important if documentation must be submitted to school districts or if you are seeing recording links to clients pertaining to only their child.

This step keeps your online tutoring sessions in quality shape with the recording feature of the virtual classroom. This is also an important step for monitoring tutor's progress when it comes to performance review time.

Step 11: Request Monitoring Notes from Tutors

In Step 11, it is very important to receive monitoring notes from tutors in a timely manner. It is recommended that you allow tutors at least 48 business hours to turn in those reports. You will need a process to manage these monitoring notes because you end up having 8-12 monitoring notes for each client.

Step 12: Share Progress With Parents

You should send out monitoring notes to clients within 72 business hours. In the event that the client attends two to three days a week, it may be more feasible to send out a brief weekly update and a detailed monthly progress report.

You may send them via mail or email. Before you do though, please ask the parents their preferred method of contact. When in doubt, send those reports via mail, preferably certified mail.

> **Expert's Advice:** I highly recommend using an online program such as Google docs or Dropbox to manage these files. Once you start getting a lot of clients, you will appreciate my advice and understand the importance and value of these notes. Monitoring notes should be used to create the monthly progress report for your clients. Let's face it...the tutor will know first-hand how a learner performs.

Step 13: Seek Feedback Regarding Your Online Tutoring Program

You will need feedback from parents, students, and tutors to truly gain insight into how to improve your online tutoring program. I strongly encourage you to use online survey programs such as survey monkey to help with managing, collecting, and analyzing data. This should be done at the very end of the learner's online tutoring program.

In this chapter, you had an opportunity to learn about the 13-step progress of working with both new and returning clients. Each of these steps will help increase your organizational practices and reputation as an effective online tutoring company.

Part III:
Applying the Lesson Framework and Building an Online Curriculum for Your Tutoring Business

CHAPTER 5
Applying the Dr. Holland-Johnson's Lesson Framework

By now, you may have discovered that tutoring lesson are not the same as classroom lessons. Of course, there will be some similarities, but there's a short window of time that must be maximized in both educational settings.

For instance, depending on the grade level, tutoring sessions can last anywhere from 30 minutes to 2 hours. Please note that I am not discussing homework help tutoring, but instructional tutoring that requires a data-driven approach. In this chapter, we will be discussing how to apply the Dr. Holland-Johnson's Lesson Framework.

The Tutoring Lesson Framework for Effective Tutoring

Before planning a tutoring session, it is very important to understand the framework that makes up an effective tutoring lesson. Let's look at the following model:

Dr.Holland-Johnson's Lesson Framework for Effective Tutoring

> Lesson Description

> Learning Objectives

> Connect Learning Objectives to Student Lives

> Introduction

> Specific Vocabulary for Tutoring Sessions

> Direct Instruction: Modeling for You

> Guided Instruction: Working for You

> Video Suggestions for Tutoring Sessions

> Independent Instruction: Working on Your Own

> Mini-Assessment

> Lesson Reflection

When it comes to the lesson description, it is very important to describe the lesson in more than one sentence. You need to share how the lesson was designed and go more into detail about the key concepts that will be explored in the tutoring session.

In terms of the *Learning Objectives*, they should only relate to the tutoring session that is stated for that particular day. You want to make sure that the learning objectives are deemed measurable [Include your lesson notes from your website here].

The third component is *Connecting Learning Objectives to Students Lives*. Studentscan learn more when they understand how the lesson or key concept are related to their own lives. This is especially true as the learner advance to secondary and post–secondary learning. You can include at least two to four real world connections depending on the concept.

The fourth component is the *Introduction*. You may decide to use the real-world connections as part of your introduction or begin to introduce the concepts in different way. Whatever you decide to do, it should be done for learner and very succinct so that most of the time can be spent during the actual tutoring instruction.

The fifth component, *Specific Vocabulary for Tutoring Session*, focus only on the vocabulary terms that will be used in the tutoring sessions. Depending on the topic, these key terms can range from 1-15 vocabulary terms. Learners do need to spend time interacting with the key terms both during and after the tutoring session.

The six component,*Direct Instruction: Modeling for You* is where the tutor will coach the learner on how to approach a certain topic. This component is very important because learners are able to observe the tutor thought process regarding the topic. A great deal of time should not be sent here as the goal is to engage the learner in the tutoring process as well. It is extremely important for the tutor to have strong content knowledge so that he or she can model effectively for their learners.

The seventh component,*Guided Instruction: Working with You* is where the learner will have an opportunity to work with you. This is a chance to have the learner practice sharing his or her strategy on solving problems related to the content presented in the tutoring session. It is extremely important to pose pivotal questions to enhance his or her critical thinking. Depending on the learner's ability to grasp the material, you may only need to work through a few questions. However, you will need to use your own professional judgment.

The eight component, *Video Suggestions for Tutoring Sessions,* are necessary to engage learners. You may decide to add a reflection question related to the short orders or you may decide to use part of the video as a teaching tool. As you are planning instructions for learners, this is something that you will need to keep in mind.

The ninth component, *Independent Instruction: Working on Your Own,* is where your learner will demonstrate that he or she has grasped the material and is ready to apply the knowledge. Depending on whether the learner has mastered the material, then he or she will be ready for the official assessment in which he or she will have to master the material with a certain percentage. Again, you will need to know when it is time to administer the mini-assessment by using your professional judgment and data-collection throughout the tutoring session.

The last component, *Lesson Reflection,* focuses on a recap of what occurred in the tutoring session. This is the perfect time to provide reflective opportunities with a few questions to help move the knowledge into long-term memory. Additionally, this is an opportunity to ask the learners any question in which they have that may still need to be addressed as it relates to the tutoring session.

CHAPTER 6
Building a Customized Online Curriculum

We are living in an era where technology changes every nano-second. Another important aspect to think about is how education is moving into uncharted territories so the need of building a customized online curriculum is paramount. In this chapter, the focus is going to be on helping you decide on what to include in your online curriculum and to implement it into your own learning organization.

What is a Customized Online Curriculum?

It's a curriculum that is electronic and can supplement an existing curriculum that may be taught face-to-face. Depending on how you want to implement your online curriculum, it will determine whether you need Customized platform or use existing online resources that can be considered supplementary.

Let's look at some of the question in which you should ask yourself about building a customized online curriculum.These questions are the following:

1. How do you plan on using online curriculum in your learning organization?

_____

_____

_____

_____

2. Will it be solely online curriculum or online supplementary curriculum to your existing face-to-face curriculum? Why or why not?

_____

_____

_____

_____

3. How do you plan on conducting a needs assessment to determine your online curriculum offerings?

_____

_____

_____

_____

4. What are the overall vision and goals for the customized online curriculum?

_____

_____

_____

_____

5. How do you plan on preparing staff for these upcoming changes?

6. How often do you plan to update the curriculum?

7. Who will be responsible for the curriculum and its life cycle? If it is you, how will you plan on managing the daily operation of your tutoring practice?

8. How do you plan on implementing pre-and post- assessment into your customized online curriculum?

9. How do you plan on implementing progress monitoring and mini-assessment into your customized online curriculum?

10. Which research-based curriculum models do you plan on using to design your online curriculum? What is your rationale for selecting this type of curriculum model?

11. What types of open education resources would you add to enhance the customized online curriculum?

12. How do you plan on using tutor-authored content?

13. What percentage of your online curriculum will be tutor-authored, commercial, and/or open educational resources?

_____
_____
_____
_____
_____

14. How do you plan on using adaptive assessment and lessons?

_____
_____
_____
_____
_____

15. What platforms do you plan on selecting to host your content for the lessons?

_____
_____
_____
_____
_____

16. How do you plan to embed a balance amount of multimedia rich content throughout the courses?

_____
_____
_____
_____
_____

17. Which national or international standards of quality for online courses and/or curriculum plan on using?

18. How do you plan on tracking student outcomes with a linkage to online content?

19. How do you plan on creating a budget to address ongoing curriculum cost and upgrades?

20. Depending on your learner organizations size, how do you plan on accounting for staffing and compensation models?

These questions and your response to those questions should help you come up with responses that will support you in building a customized online curriculum for your learning organization. As you are answering these questions and another question comes up, then please email me and let me know. Perhaps, I could share some more food for thought questions with you.

Dr. Holland's Advice

You will find that your online curriculum will need to be updated frequently, but that's okay because you are working with students based upon their needs. After all, that's what tutoring is all about. In some settings, it is called personalize learning, but at the root of it comes tutoring. Therefore, you may discover a pattern of topics in which students may need more assistance and you may decide to develop additional curriculum around those topics.

This chapter was designed only to help you reflect on building a customized online curriculum. I hope that you found the reflection questions helpful to you.

Part IV:
Data-Driven Tutoring in the Virtual Classroom

CHAPTER 7
Conducting Online Tutoring Sessions and Writing Monitoring Notes for Clients

You have just gotten either your first client or have been in business for a while. At this point, it is time to analyze how to conduct your tutoring sessions. It seems like it should be a piece of cake, but there is a little more to it than you may first believe. In this section, we will be discussing how to develop procedures for opening and closing tutoring sessions. Before we do this, we need to take a look at the Tutoring Framework for Effective Tutoring.

The Tutoring Framework for Effective Tutoring

Before engaging in tutoring sessions, it is very important to understand the framework that makes up an effective tutoring session. Let's take a look at the Dr. Alicia Holland's Tutoring Framework for Effective Tutoring Model on the next page.

Dr. Alicia Holland's Tutoring Framework for Effective Tutoring Model

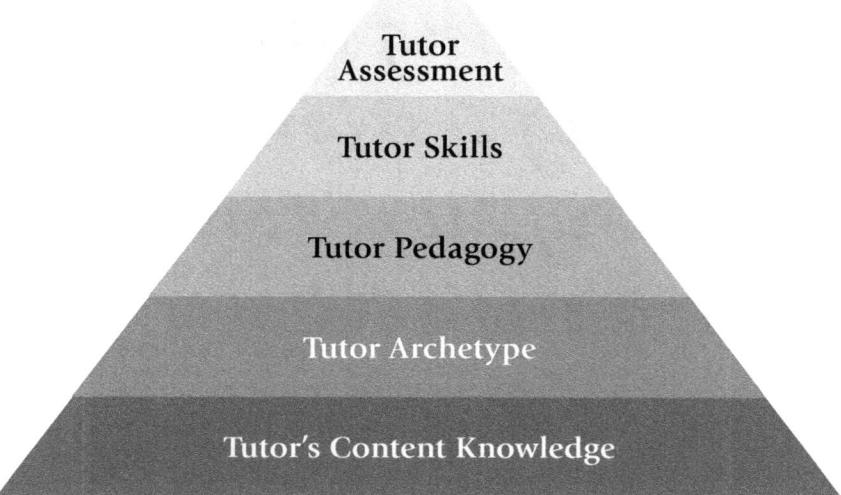

When it comes to the *Tutor's Content Knowledge*, it is very important to understand that a tutor's content knowledge is the foundation of the tutoring session because he or she knows the direction the tutoring session needs to flow. In this figure, it is at the bottom layer because it represents the basis in which the tutoring pyramid needs to be strong. In other words, tutors need to have strong content knowledge to be able to help others learn and grow.

In terms of the *Tutor Archetype*, they are the various types of tutor styles a tutor can utilize to help their learners. Dr. Alicia Holland (2010) identifies and describes three types of tutors: homework tutors, instructional tutors, and strategic tutors (p. 74). These tutor types are associated with working with K-12 learners (Holland-Johnson, A., 2010).

As mentioned in the previous chapter, Harootunian and Quinn (2008) identify and describe three tutor archetypes that work best with high school and adult learners. These three tutor archetypes are the following: (a) the pragmatist; (b) the architect; and (c) the surveyor (p. 15).

The *Tutor Pedagogy* is also paramount for effective tutoring. Once tutors have determined the type of tutoring they need for their learners, it is time to focus on "how" they will tutor the learners. This is where instructional strategies and learning theories are important in planning tutoring sessions for learners. This step goes beyond looking at learning objectives, but really focusing on how to reach learners using best practices.

Tutoring Skills are also valued in this tutoring framework for effective tutoring. At this point, tutors are ready to deliver the instruction to learners. It is the job of the tutor to engage learners and deliver instruction using all learning modalities to increase the chances of learners retaining the information. When learners retain the information, they are able to apply it to a new situation or current learning situation.

Last but not least, the *Tutor Assessment* is there to determine if the learner has benefitted from effective tutoring. In other words, once the tutor and learner have worked together on concepts, the tutor should provide assessments to measure the learner's mastery of skills. These assessments should not be comprehension questions only, but a variety of questions that will enable the learner to truly reflect their knowledge. Tutors must implement an assessment plan that will capture immediate and future retention of the learners' knowledge. Tutors who have a strong content knowledge will be able to create or provide various types of assessments to meet the learners' needs and depict a true assessment of the learners' knowledge and skills.

> **Expert's Advice:** When you study this framework for effective tutoring, please take the time to reflect on why I focused on the improvement of tutoring your skills at the beginning of the book. Since you see that the tutor's knowledge is crucial, it is very important to be a life-long learner so that your clients can reap the benefits.

> **Expert's Advice:** *(continued)*
>
> When you take some time out to study your competition, what do you notice? Are they steadily getting clients because of low prices or is it because the tutor delivers results for his or her clients? I will let you be the judge. My challenge to you is to always consider your approach to learning as a life-long journey. The truth is that we all learn something new each day and the same occurs in the tutoring industry.

How to Open Tutoring Sessions

Each tutoring session should open with a greeting to make a connection with the client. After a connection has been made, you should communicate with the client what he or she will be learning and address any goals that have been set, whether the goals are for this session or another session. By communicating the session's objective(s), the tutor allows the client to be prepared for what the session will cover. Imagine going to the dentist's office if the dentist never told you what was going to go on in that visit. The most you may know about the visit is that your teeth will be cleaned. If any other procedures were performed, wouldn't you be upset? The same is true for your clients; they want to be in the know about their learning.

Sample Opening of a Tutoring Session

Tutor: Hi, my name is Zoey, and I will be your tutor today. How was your day?

Student: My day was okay. I lost my favorite pendant in gym. Other than that, I am good. Here's my report card.

> *Tutor:* In today's session, we are going to look at describing quadrilaterals according to their characteristics. Have you worked with quadrilaterals before?
>
> *Student:* Yes, I remember working with squares and rectangles a lot in fourth and fifth grade. Isn't that what quadrilaterals are?
>
> *Tutor:* Well, you have identified two quadrilaterals. The mathematical definition is: Quadrilaterals are polygons that have four sides. It's great to know that you already know about squares and rectangles, because you will find yourself having fun learning the rest of the quadrilaterals. I noticed that you met your goal of receiving at least a B in your math class. Based upon your report card grades, you are doing well in all your classes. You got an A in your math class. Great job; keep up the good work.

Once you have opened the session, it is time to personalize the session and begin working on your client's specific needs. We will talk about ways to praise clients during the tutoring sessions later in this chapter.

How to Close Tutoring Sessions

As with any presentation, you want to end it with a sense that your audience has gotten the importance of the message. The same is true for a tutoring session; a tutoring session should be brought to an educationally sound close. What does "educationally sound" mean? This means that you should not be in the middle of a question and abruptly stop the session because of time constraints. This leaves the session open, and neither you nor the client can determine what the next steps may be for the next session. On the other hand, if there was a written assessment or monitoring notes, then the tutor should be able to pick up where he or she and the client left of, and the client has an idea of the topics that will be covered in the next tutoring session. Please keep in mind that all sessions are not going to be the same and will eventually need to come to an end.

Sample Closing of a Tutoring Session

Tutor: You did a great job on your homework. Now, let me grade your mini-assessment on comparing fractions. While I look at these five questions, take a moment to stretch, or you may play Math Man [an online educational game that allows individuals to practice their multiplication skills] on the computer.

Student: Okay, I think I will stretch as I am standing up to go play Math Man.

Tutor: Okay, Mike. You have five minutes, and then I need you to come back to the table so we can discuss your results and end the session. (Five minutes have passed.)

Student: I'm back. What did I make on my assessment?

Tutor: You scored a six out of eight, which is 75 percent. This score lets me know that we can move on to the next topic. You did a great job today. Do you have any questions? What did you learn in today's session?

Student: No, I do not have any questions. I learned that I can cross- multiply or find a common denominator to compare fractions.

Tutor: If you do not have any further questions, then this session has ended, and if there's still time, you can continue working on your multiplication skills until your ride comes. See you next week.

Student: Okay. Bye and thank you.

> **Expert's Advice:** As you may already know, the beginning and ending of a tutoring session are important. I must admit that when I first started my tutoring business I had to learn how to start a tutoring session, even though I had teaching experience. Tutoring sessions open differently from a lesson that would be taught in class. Please understand that clients feed off your energy. After all, you are running a business (one that you love), and clients want to learn from an energetic and positive person. The main concept about opening and closing tutoring sessions is that the feelings experienced during this time will affect: (1) the climate during the tutoring session, and (2) whether or not the client will be motivated to come again. Think about it—would you want to return to a business where no one greets you or appears jovial? Would you want to return to a business that didn't thank you or show you that you are important? Well, your clients don't either... that's why it is important to devise a strategy for opening and closing your tutoring sessions.

Structure of Tutoring Sessions

A typical tutoring session, whether you are a homework, instructional, or strategic tutor, would last forty-five minutes to two hours. Some clients prefer to work in two-hour increments to complete homework and other assignments. Oftentimes this works for motivated and older clients. This allows them to devote focused time to homework. Here are suggested pacing schedules for a typical tutoring session lasting one hour or two hours.

- 5-10 minutes   Open session
- 25 minutes   Subject 1
- 25 minutes   Subject 2
- 25 minutes   Subject 3
- 25 minutes   Subject 4
- 5-10 minutes   Close session

Please keep in mind that tutoring sessions should be tailored to your client's needs. For instance, if you have a client with special needs, more time may be spent on one or two subjects, depending on his or her comfort level. In any event, these pacing schedules only serve as a starting point for structuring tutoring sessions.

Conducting Online Tutoring Sessions and Writing Monitoring Notes

If you have been tutoring for some time in person, you have a general idea of how a tutoring session should open. In your quest of becoming an online tutor, you will experience many online tutoring platforms. No matter the platform, you still need to know how to conduct online tutoring sessions. In this chapter, I will share with you strategies to have a productive tutoring session.

Opening an Online Tutoring Session

The first step is to get online and get connected into the virtual classroom. Once this is done, it is time to get set up so that valuable tutoring session time is not wasted on organization. Here's a chart to help summary the steps that should be taken when setting up for an online tutoring session.

Importance of Early Arrival in the Virtual Classroom

If you are using a virtual classroom platform, you will need to enter the classroom at least 10-15 minutes before your client so that you can set up your lesson. Typically, tutors upload necessary files to the whiteboard and post a welcome message for the client.

Posting a Welcome Message in the Virtual Classroom

The welcome message should be warm and make the learner feel at ease when working online with you. The welcome message should also include the learning objective(s), tutoring session agenda, and a quick reminder to make sure that he or she types in either his or her first and last name.

Below is a sample welcome message:

Welcome to Our Online Tutoring Session, [Insert Learner's Name]!

Please take a moment and type both your first and last name.

Please solve the problem in the chat window. You can show your work on the whiteboard.

Today's Tutoring Session Agenda

1 Problem Solving Strategies
2 Solving Word Problems
3 Mini-Assessment
4 Closure

Look forward to working with you,
Your Favorite Online Tutor

This should be written at the beginning of every tutoring session prior to the learner entering the classroom. That way, the learner can spend time learning what he or she will be learning for that specific tutoring session and it will be using tutoring session time wisely.

Posting Warm-Up Questions in the Virtual Classroom

It's always a good idea to get your learner warmed-up with some sort of problem or writing prompt. It should not be a challenge, but it is a good way to assess whether the learner has the prerequisite skills necessary to be engaged in the current tutoring session. Depending on your content area, this will depend on how the warm-up may look for each learner. This warm-up should not take more than 10 minutes and should segue into the topic(s) that will be learned in the tutoring session.

Uploading Files in the Virtual Classroom

When it comes to uploading files, this can range from a warm-up activity, mini-assessments, or even a presentation that is used for the tutoring session. It's always a great idea to use visuals to help your learners with learning the material. Depending on the type of file that is being updated, it will determine the amount of time that will need to be spent performing this task. Just a heads up, some files can lock up the virtual classroom while loading so you do want to make sure that you arrive ahead of the tutoring session so that it will already be uploaded for future references in the tutoring session.

Checking the Virtual Classroom Settings

Another important task to check before the tutoring session is the virtual classroom settings, especially when it comes to audio and the microphone. Once the learner enters the tutoring session, you may have to ask him or her if they can hear you and vice versa. Once that is done, the tutoring session should be ready to begin without any concerns. It is wise to let the learner know that if either you or her gets kicked out of the virtual classroom that the expectation is to log back in to continue the tutoring session. If that does happen, then this technical difficulty should not count towards the tutoring session time.

Let's look at a sample opening of an online tutoring session to see how this works together with the welcome message and so forth.

(Online Tutor Arrived 15 minutes early to the online tutoring session and typed the welcome message.)

Online Tutor [Mrs. Amaiya]: Welcome to Our Online Tutoring Session, Trinity!

Please take a moment and type both your first and last name.

Please solve the problem in the chat window. You can show your work on the whiteboard.

Look forward to working with you, Your Favorite Online Tutor.

(Online Learner enters the classroom 15 minutes later; Online Learner types response in the chat OR speak to the online tutor using a microphone.)

Online Learner [Trinity]: Hi, Mrs. Amaiya. I will solve that problem right now. May I have a new whiteboard?

(Mrs. Amaiya writes the objectives for the tutoring session in both the chat and the whiteboard; she speaks to Trinity now about it.)

Mrs. Amaiya: In today's session, we are going to solve word problems by using addition, subtraction, multiplication, and division. What are some problem solving strategies that you have used before?

Trinity: Well, sometimes I draw a picture, but mostly I guess my answer after working the problem and eliminating answer choices.

Mrs. Amaiya:	Okay, thanks for being honest. Did you know that there are six different problem-solving strategies to use in math? Let's look at them on the whiteboard and we will watch a short video clip of how they are used when solving problems in the real world.

(The actual tutoring lesson begins.)

> **Expert's Advice:** Mrs. Amaiya did a very good job of setting up her online tutoring session before the student arrived. As you can see, this is a lot of information to try to set up, and it will take about the first 15 minutes of a session to get started. Rather than take time away from the learner, I highly recommend that tutors arrive in their tutoring sessions at least 10-15 minutes before it starts. Also, during the tutoring session, Mrs. Amaiya could use both verbal and emoticons to show praise for Trinity's progress.

Now let's take a look at a sample closing of a tutoring session.

(Trinity took her mini-assessment, and now it is time to bring the session to a close in an organized fashion.)

Online Tutor [Mrs. Amaiya]:	In the chatbox, you should see a question that asks you to summarize what was learned today. Please type your response.

(Online Learner, Trinity, recalls the mini-assessment, which happened to be a math essay question. The math essay question was the following: Rayneisha is a new student in your class. She really does not understand how to solve triangles. How would you explain to Rayneisha how to classify triangles and find the area of triangles? Please show your work.)

Mrs. Amaiya: What did you learn today? Do you still have any questions? Are you sure?

Trinity: I learned how to solve word problems and classify triangles. No, I do not have any questions. I just got some make-up work that needs to be done at school.

Mrs. Amaiya: If you do not have any further questions, then this session has ended. See you next week, and it was a pleasure working with you.

Trinity: Okay, Bye Mrs. Amaiya and thanks for your help.

(The tutoring session ends and both Trinity and Mrs. Amaiya logs out of the virtual classroom.)

Expert's Advice: Mrs. Amaiya allowed Trinity to ask any additional questions if she had any. It seems like Trinity passed her mini-assessment because Mrs. Amaiya did not take the time to discuss it at the close of the tutoring session. It could also mean that time was running out and the mini-assessment would need to be graded and it would be discussed at the next session. It is very unclear. However, this is a sample of how online tutoring sessions should be closed. The goal is not to re-introduce topics, but to get a good understanding of what was learned in the tutoring session and to provide an opportunity to the learner regarding additional topics that may need to be addressed at a future tutoring session. Most importantly, the student was able to reflect upon their learning.

Structure of Online Tutoring Sessions

A typical online tutoring session can last anywhere from 45 minutes to 120 minutes. Depending on the client's needs and attention span, it will determine the length of the tutoring session.

Here are suggested pacing schedules for a typical tutoring session ranging from 45 minutes to 120 minutes:

45-minutes Tutoring (Sessions	60-minutes Tutoring Sessions	90-minutes Tutoring Sessions	120-minutes Tutoring Sessions
• Open session (5 mins.) • Subject 1 (25 mins.) • Mini-Assessment (10 mins.) • Close Session (5 mins.)	• Open session (5 mins.) • Subject 1 (35 mins.) • Mini-Assessment (15 mins.) • Close Session (5 mins.)	• Open session (5 mins.) • Subject 1 (25 mins.) • Subject 2 (25 mins.) • Guided Practice (15 mins.) • Mini-Assessment (15 mins.) • Close Session (5 mins.)	• Open session (5 mins.) • Subject 1 (25 mins.) • Subject 2 (25 mins.) • Subject 3 (25 mins.) • Subject 4 (25 mins.) • Problem Solving (25 mins.) • Mini-Assessment (25 mins.) • Close Session (5 mins.)

Please keep in mind that all online tutoring sessions should be tailored to your client's needs. For instance, if you have a client with special needs, more time may be spent on one or two subjects, depending on his or her comfort level. In any event, these pacing schedules only serve as a starting point for structuring tutoring sessions.

Writing Monitoring Notes for Clients during Tutoring Sessions

Have you ever gone to your doctor several months after a visit? What happened? I am guessing that your doctor was able to recall the last session by looking at your chart. Did you know that he was looking at his notes in your file? The same process applies with your clients in your tutoring practice—you keep notes on your client's progress.

Monitoring notes serve three purposes:

1. They are used to help keep track of the client's progress.
2. They are used to help keep you fully informed about instructional decisions.
3. They are used to keep clients (and parents) informed of their (or their child's) progress. (Holland-Johnson, 2010, p. 92).

Whether you tutor face-to-face or online, it is best practice to keep monitoring notes on all clients as a way to provide data-driven tutoring services.

Components of Online Monitoring Notes

There are eight components that are useful for both the clients and tutors. These components are listed below:

- Student and Session Information
- Vocabulary
- Attitude/Effort
- Tutor Observation
- Learner's Progress
- Next Instructional Steps
- Tutor Recommendation
- Tutor's Rating of the Online Tutoring Session

Student and Session Information

For every monitoring note, the tutor should be listed, along with the student who is being tutored. Other session information such as the date and time that the session takes place and the learning objective(s) slated for the tutoring session should be listed in this session as well.

Vocabulary

It is helpful to know the type of terminology that is being used in each tutoring session. This helps both the clients and tutors when it comes time to send out progress reports. Most importantly, this is a great way to show that grade level vocabulary is being used in tutoring sessions rather than slang for content-related vocabulary.

Attitude/Effort

The Attitude/Effort is considered nonacademic factors in tutoring sessions. However, this type of data offers vital information regarding the atmosphere of the tutoring session and how committed the learner was to the tutoring session. In other words, it helps to better understand why a learner made progress or not.

Tutor Observation

Tutor observations are the tutor's informal assessment of how the learner is performing in the session and how the content helped the student. This is another type of qualitative data that adds value to monitoring notes and hold tutor's accountable for their tutoring sessions.

Learner's Progress

This component will detail how the learner performed during the session.

"It should be in narrative form, but succinct, so that you are able to get an overall picture of the client's strengths and weaknesses during the session. If any mini-assessments are given at the end of the session, you should include the results. For example, a client named Shirley got three out of four test questions correct, which is 75 percent. As a result, Shirley has mastered how to compare fractions using concrete objects. A short paragraph (three to five sentences) should be included in this section for each subject that you are working on. For instance, if you are working on math and reading skills, there should be a section clearly labeled "Math and Reading," followed by the name of the activity or skill so that clients can understand the information. This is important because parents or guardians or adult clients are responsible for payment. Once this section has been completed, you should list the next instructional step(s)" (Holland-Johnson, 2010, p. 94).

Next Instructional Steps

This component is dedicated to determining the next instructional step. This is where information regarding how a learner has mastered a particular learning objective will come in handy. On the other hand, this is the section in which tutors should definitely document what are the next instructional steps for learners who did not master the content presented in the online tutoring session. This information is typically shared in progress reports that are sent out to clients and parents, if the clients are minors.

Tutor Recommendation

Since the tutor is working with the learner, it is very important to get their professional recommendation regarding the student's next step. This information is typically shared in progress reports that are sent out to clients and parents, if the clients are minors.

Tutor's Rating of the Online Tutoring Session

It is important to allow the tutor to rate the online tutoring session since students will have an opportunity to do the same thing. This is a great way to go back and look at the tutor's performance in the virtual classroom. In addition, this is a great way to find out about any technical difficulties whether it be on either the student's or tutor's computer. The bottom line is that it is documented in the monitoring notes if anything transpires.

Now that you have some strategies to help you with conducting quality online tutoring sessions, let your spirit guide you when you are starting and operating your online tutoring business.

Praising Student Motivation and Performance in Tutoring Sessions

How many people do you know who would turn down praise? Have you ever been praised for a job well done? What does praise mean to you?

According to the online Merriam-Webster dictionary (2012), to praise is "To express a favorable judgment of" (para. 1).

Here are a few questions to consider when praising clients:

1. How do your clients respond to praise?

_____

_____

_____

_____

2. Do you use verbal or nonverbal praises? How do you use them?

_____

_____

3. Have you thought about a reward system? Why or why not?

4. How does praise look in tutoring?

Tutors may choose to praise students either verbally or nonverbally. Verbal praises are thoughts spoken in real time. For example, "Nice job" or "You are doing great" are verbal praises. In tutoring, these types of praises are warranted, but praises should be more specific for individual clients' achievements. Imagine that you have received praise from your boss, but he only said to you, "Nice job!" How would that feel? Initially, you would be feeling good inside to the point that you were glowing. Once your brain had processed the information, however, you would be asking yourself, "What did I do a nice job on?" The point is that you are spending time and energy on trying to figure out what your boss is praising you for when you should be putting the energy toward your job responsibilities. Do you want your clients to have the same experience? Praise does not mean anything if it is given either in isolation or too often. Praise works best when it is linked to a specific task or behavior. Gonzalez-Mena (2009) says it best:

They [Adults] replace honest feedback with constant overblown praise. Praise is no cure for low self-esteem. All it does is create a need for the child to look to the adult for a judgment of everything he does—if you overdo praise, your words become meaningless (p. 211).

SCENARIO: *"Yes, You Can"*

Daisy, a tenth-grade student who has dyslexia and dysgraphia, has been working with a private reading tutor named Josh. Daisy has difficulty comprehending complex information, especially if the information pertains to specific subject areas. After Josh worked with Daisy for five months, she finally passed the tenth-grade reading test. When he heard the news, Josh called Daisy's parents and congratulated them. He also talked with Daisy, telling her, "Daisy, you have been working so hard on your reading skills and all your hard work paid off. Congratulations, and I am so proud of you. Keep up the great work."

From that point on, Daisy continued to work with Josh once a week and continued to improve her reading skills and confidence in learning.

1. Is there anything that you would have done differently? Why or why not?

_____
_____
_____
_____

2. How do you praise your clients in your tutoring services?

_____
_____
_____
_____

> **Expert's Advice:** Josh did a great job with being specific in his praise of Daisy. The praise actually worked in this situation. Specific praise can go a long way with people if it is genuine and consistent.

Reward Systems in Tutoring

Clients need to be rewarded for engagement and performance so that they are able to feel confident about their learning. There are several strategies that can be used to reward clients. One strategy that can be used as a reward system is the ticket system, while other strategies that can enhance a reward system include both gift cards and small gifts.

Using the Tickets to Enhance Your Reward System in Your Tutoring Practice

The ticket system should be designed to reward desired performance and effort. Tickets should be given each session, but no more than five tickets should be handed out in a single one-hour session. This is because you do not want clients to expect to receive rewards for every little task. Think about your own reward credit cards, customer reward cards (e.g., store reward cards), or merit raises. Do you constantly receive rewards without working hard for them? If you do, please let me know so that I can sign up to receive these rewards as well!

Here's a sample ticket system and the way it works.

Students can earn up to five tickets in a session and can cash their tickets in at any time.

Students can earn tickets the following ways:

- 100 percent on a mini-assessment = three tickets
- 90 percent to 99 percent on a mini-assessment = two tickets

- 80 percent to 89 percent on a mini-assessment = one ticket
- Motivation = discretion of tutor
- Participation = discretion of tutor
- Good grades in school (per six or nine weeks) = ten tickets
- Turning in all assignments on time (must have teacher's signatures) = five tickets
- Good test grades = three tickets per test in every subject

What Can You Buy with Your Tickets?

- Five tickets: small items, such as pens, pencils, erasers, stickers.
- Ten tickets: medium items, such as playing cards, extra time on the computer to play game of choice, other items that are donated.
- Fifteen tickets: large items, such as games that are donated.
- Twenty-five tickets: free movie ticket of choice, other items that are donated.
- One hundred tickets: large items that are donated, such as free iTunes card, or $25 gift card.
- Five hundred tickets: iPod, video game of choice, or $50 gift card.
- One thousand tickets: mini-laptop computer, video game system of choice, or $100 gift card.
- Monthly drawing for a prize: at the end of each month (TBD).

Expert's Advice: I must admit that at first I was a little hesitant to add such a system to reward desired performance and effort. In fact, for the first three years, I did not have an official reward system. I instituted it because a parent had recommended it and supplied me with costly items that students could purchase with their earned tickets. When I introduced the reward

> **Expert's Advice:** *(continued)*
>
> system to both parents and clients, the response was overwhelmingly positive. At that moment, I realized that I was moving in the right direction. The hard parts were determining the frequency of when to give out tickets, management of the ticket system, and choosing criteria for the system.
>
> I strongly recommend that you explain to clients (and parents) the rationale of the ticket system and link it to research. That way there will not be any misunderstandings, and the expectations will be clear. This can be done in person, but I strongly suggest that you send it via e-mail or place it in your newsletter to your clients. If you use this system appropriately, you will be content with the results.

Using Small Gifts and Gift Cards to Enhance Your Reward System in Your Tutoring Practice

When it comes to providing gifts to clients, it is very important to make sure that you follow a few guidelines that will keep your tutoring reputation out of trouble.

Below are a few guidelines to ensure that you are making the right decisions in the best interest of your clients.

Inexpensive Gift	Education-Related	Specific Timeframe

When it comes to the first guideline, *Inexpensive Gift*, you really have to be careful. You are in business to help others. Therefore, you main goal should not be to entice clients to sign up with you for tutoring services because you offer a special gift. As a result, you should make sure that the value does not exceed $50. Instead, you want to make sure that you provide an incentive so that clients will show up to their tutoring sessions. The fact that they will receive a gift valued at $50 is a blessing. Honestly, there are a great deal of gifts that can be purchased and still be meaningful to your clients.

The second guideline, *Education-Related*, is also important for your tutoring business credibility. You do not want to find yourself giving out gifts that you cannot justify on how it will help your client's education. Therefore, you need to research gifts that are beneficial to your clients.

The third guideline, *Providing a Specific Timeframe*, lets the client know how they can be eligible for their free gift and when it will be available to redeem. Typically, once clients are enrolled, then they are notified that they are eligible depending on the completion of their tutoring program.

Once students have completed their program, then they will be notified when gifts have been mailed out or can be picked up at the office.

> **Expert's Advice:** I provided you with some good guidelines for keeping within the integrity of your tutoring program. If you plan on expanding your tutoring practice, then you will need to keep prices at or below $50, especially if you plan on working with the government. They frown on tutoring businesses who offer big-ticket gifts such as iPads and computers. Honestly, I do not blame them because our job is to educate, not bribe people. However, you can offer to purchase learning tools for your clients, which is a totally different story.
>
> I think that a rewards system should be viewed as an added benefit of why clients choose you, and you should treat it as such.

> **Expert's Advice** *(continued)*
>
> In terms of gift cards, you need to follow the same guidelines. If you are out of ideas, ask your clients by finding out their interests and favorite books. With this type of information, you cannot go wrong—it does not get any better than that.

Writing Monitoring Notes for Clients during Tutoring Sessions

Let's take a look at a tutoring situation with Amy, a reading tutor.

SCENARIO: "How is My Child Doing?" "He's Doing Fine."

Amy, a reading tutor, has been tutoring for two years now. She only works with three clients per year because she is only supplementing her income. Each of her clients has been with her at least a year. She meets each of them at their home. On one particular Tuesday, one of the clients asked how his son was doing. Rather than give detailed notes, Amy communicated his progress verbally.

Two weeks later, the parent attended a parent/teacher conference and discovered that his son was performing poorly in reading. The parent did not have any documentation from Amy to show the teacher that he was making progress. Immediately, the parent called Amy and informed him of his grades. In addition, the parent fired Amy as his child's tutor because there was not any written evidence that she was an effective tutor.

1. What could Amy have done differently in this situation?

2. How would you have handled the situation with this parent?

3. From the parent's perspective, do you think that he made the right decision? Why or why not?

> **Expert's Advice:** This could have been prevented by taking monitoring notes. Typically, students who are having problems in school will perform better in tutoring because of the setting. This was an opportunity for Amy to show her skills as an effective tutor by being proactive. Parents need to know how their child is performing.
>
> You also have to be careful because there are some parents out there that will sue you for professional liability so you it is always in your best interest to have insurance and document like crazy.

Imagine submitting an assignment to your teacher, and she does not provide feedback. How would you feel? Or, imagine that you applied for a loan and did not receive feedback on why you were denied. How would you feel? That is how clients feel when they do not have updates on either their progress or their child's progress. Monitoring notes serve three purposes.

1. They help keep track of the client's progress.
2. They help keep you fully informed about instructional decisions.
3. They keep clients (and parents) informed of their (or their child's) progress.

Monitoring notes allow tutors and parents to have documentation of student learning. There are some components that must be included in order for monitoring notes to be useful to both clients and the tutor. These components are the following: (1) student and session information; (2) effort/attitude; (3) student progress; (4) next instructional step(s); (5) parent resources, if any; and (5) upcoming sessions/request for parent-tutor conference.

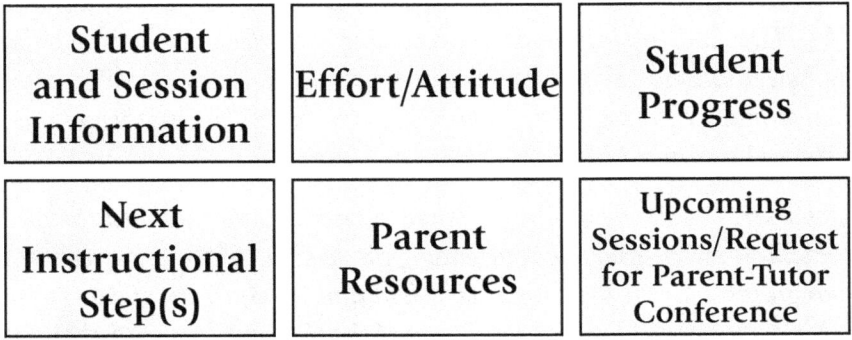

Student and Session Information

Student and session information provide critical information to help identify clients and keep records accurate. The student information should include the client's name and date of birth, though I only use the date of birth when I have more than one client with the same first and last name. The session information should clearly state the subjects tutored and the date/time of the tutoring session. All this information should be written at the beginning of the monitoring notes for easy reference.

Effort/Attitude

This component is extremely important for tutoring sessions. It provides vital information to help you improvise for the tutoring session. In other words, when a client is happy and motivated to learn, then your energy will be high and the tutoring session will go well. On the other hand, if the client is not happy about coming to the session, then you will have to be creative to get the session going. Please understand that clients are paying for your services, and they expect you to provide quality services to them, despite the fact that their child does not want to meet with you.

SCENARIO: "I Don't Wanna Be Here—Take Me Away, Now!"

Ethan, a fifth grader who has attention-deficit hyperactivity disorder (ADHD) and an information-processing disorder, just learned that he had to attend private tutoring in math. Ethan also attended after-school math tutoring at his school twice a week. His mother found a tutor online named Matt.

Upon arriving at the tutoring session, Ethan's mother warned the tutor that Ethan was upset about attending the session. Matt, a novice tutor, was grateful for the alert because he had time to adjust the opening of his session with Ethan. At the beginning of the tutoring session, Ethan told Matt that he was mad because he was not able to play his video game during his free time because he had to come see him for tutoring. The session did continue, but Matt had to link the lesson to Ethan's favorite sport—football. Ethan had joined the community flag football team and would have his first game the following week. To Matt' advantage, he used that information to increase Ethan's motivation for the tutoring session. This strategy worked, resulting in a productive tutoring session.

1. If you were in Matt's situation, how would you have handled the situation?

_____
_____
_____
_____
_____

2. What type of recommendation would you provide to parents regarding scheduling their child during extra-curricular activities?

_____
_____
_____
_____
_____

Student Progress

This component will detail how the client performed during the session. It should be in narrative form, but succinct, so that you are able to get an overall picture of the client's strengths and weaknesses during the session. If any mini-assessments are given at the end of the session, you should include the results. For example, a client named Shirley got three out of four test questions correct, which is 75 percent. As a result, Shirley has mastered how to compare fractions using concrete objects.

A short paragraph (three to five sentences) should be included in this section for each subject that you are working on. For instance, if you are working on math and reading skills, there should be a section clearly labeled "Math and Reading," followed by the name of the activity or skill so that clients can understand the information. This is important because parents or guardians or adult clients are responsible for payment. Once this section has been completed, you should list the next instructional step(s).

Next Instructional Step(s)

In this section, you should put the next steps for clients, which will be determined based upon their performance in the session. In other words, if the client has mastered a skill, then he or she should progress to the next skill indicated on the instructional plan. On the other hand, if a client has not mastered a concept, there should be an opportunity to revisit the concept either in the same session, given that time permits, or in the next tutoring session. Once this section has been completed, you should list additional resources for parents or adult clients.

Parent Resources

Parents and adult clients are always looking for additional resources to help their child to practice a skill at home. As their private tutor, you should be committed to providing services beyond tutoring sessions. As Maya Angelou puts it, "I've learned that people will forget what you said, people will forget what you did, but people will never forget how you made them feel." In other words, people will remember your services because of how you made them feel. Therefore, it is crucial to provide quality tutoring sessions, and excellent customer service will keep clients coming or referring others to you. Depending on your relationship with your clients, they will let you know if they need additional assistance at home. Some clients, however, are afraid to ask for additional resources because they may fear that it will cost more money. By providing additional resources, you are empowering clients to further their studies in their targeted areas.

Upcoming Sessions/Request for Parent-Tutor Conference

This section lends itself to reminding clients about their upcoming sessions so that they can make note of them. While this section provides a reminder, it is also a good idea to send an e-mail or text message or make a phone call to help clients remember their sessions. In addition, this section can be used to request parent-tutor conferences. In any event, monitoring notes allow for both clients and tutors to stay "in the know" about their needs and appointments.

> **Expert's Advice:** Monitoring notes can be considered part of the lifeblood of your tutoring business because they are so valuable. If you supply your clients with detailed monitoring notes, they will feel (and have proof) that your services are helping them or their child. In addition, if you have the intention of expanding your business or applying to professional tutoring organizations, then it is in your best interest to provide thorough monitoring notes. After all, you are accountable for the client's learning while he or she is receiving your tutoring services.
>
> When it comes to working as a homework tutor, you still need to document progress. This is done by taking monitoring notes, just like you would if you assumed the role of other types of tutors.
>
> The bottom line is that monitoring notes are considered data driven because it helps tell the story of a learner's academic situation. For instance, both tutors and parents are able to review the learner's (and their child's) progress over time. Therefore, it is very important to understand that monitoring notes capture both quantitative and qualitative data. Nevertheless, monitoring notes are considered a great tool to help understand and improve each learner's academic achievement.

Using Tutoring Session Time Cards for Tutoring Sessions

How do you know when a learner is out of tutoring sessions? Each school year, it is very important to keep track of the number of sessions that a client has attended. You may be wondering what type of information should be kept on a session card. Don't worry. I will share that with you.

The items that should be collected on the tutoring session time cards are listed below.

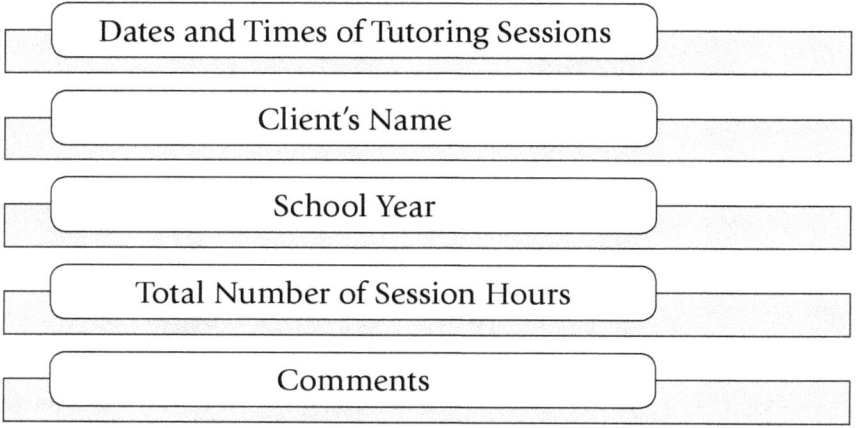

1. <u>Dates and Time of Tutoring Sessions</u>: This can be done in semesters, including the summer semester or in months of the year. Depending on how you want to display this information, you can add both. Whatever you decide, it should also include the specific day and time of the tutoring session.

2. <u>Client's Name</u>: You need to have the client's name or reference code listed to adequately document and file the learner's progress.

3. <u>School Year</u>: This is important if this is a returning client from a previous school year.

4. Total Number of Session Hours: You want to have this information readily available so that you can collect data on when clients are typically enrolled in your tutoring practice.

5. Comments: This section comes in handy if you need to document when payment is due again for services. Any comments listed in this section should pertain to the client and the tutoring sessions.

> **Expert's Advice:** Tutoring session cards are great for many reasons. After working with many clients, many parents call the office regarding the next session or payment for tutoring sessions. Also, they may need to reschedule a session or there was a session cancellation. Whatever the reason, tutoring session cards are the solution.
>
> Last but not least, please print them on cardstock and staple them to their file folder. If you run an online tutoring business, you will still need to do the same process because you may not always be in front of your computer when parents call about tutoring session changes.

Providing Student's Additional Practice After Tutoring Sessions

After working with clients, you may discover that they will need additional practice after tutoring sessions. Depending on how frequently the learner attends sessions, it will also depend on how you will assign student's additional practice. No matter the situation, you should follow a few guidelines to ensure that this additional practice benefits the learner.

Below are some guidelines to follow when providing student's additional practice after tutoring sessions:

| Clear Directions | Recommended Schedule | Due Date |

| Signature Box | Tutor Comments |

1. **Provide Clear Directions:** You have to understand that you will not be present when the learner is completing the work.

2. **Include a Recommended Schedule:** You need to let the learner know how to pace himself or herself. For example, if you provide five learning activities, then you should stress the importance of completing one learning activity per day and explain your rationale in a kid-friendly fashion.

3. **Highlight the Due Date:** You want to communicate when the tutoring practice packet is due. That way, there are not any surprises.

4. **Add a Parent/Guardian Signature Box:** When working with K-12 learners, you should always keep the parent both informed and engaged. That way, they also share the responsibility of ensuring that their child is completing the tutoring packet.

5. **Provide Tutor Comments:** You should always leave tutor comments to indicate what is going on with the packet. This type of feedback should be about the tutoring practice packet only, not the actual student work. Examples of comments can include that the parent did not sign or the packet was turned in late or incomplete.

By following these guidelines, you are able to properly assign additional practice for your clients.

> **Expert's Advice:** Tutoring practice packets are great to supplement tutoring sessions. However, you may not use them a lot during the academic school year. I found a lot of success with them during summer tutoring sessions.
>
> If you are working with home-schooled students, then you will use these packets a lot to ensure that students are getting the appropriate amount of practice to master the skill.
>
> You can find these forms and additional resources at <u>www.becomingabettertutorblog.com</u> to help with your tutoring business needs.

In this chapter, you learned how to open and close tutoring sessions and how to structure your tutoring sessions. Also, you learned the value of praise in tutoring sessions and how to write monitoring notes for clients to document their progress. Last but not least, you had an opportunity to learn about the Tutoring Framework for Effective Tutoring and how to use both session cards and tutoring practice packets with your clients. In the next chapter, you will take what you have learned about tutoring into the classroom.

CHAPTER 8
Determining the Type of Tutor You Will Need to Be for Each Tutoring Session

What type of tutor are you? Before you can develop an instructional plan for your client, it is important to identify the type of tutor you will need to be to meet your clients' needs. Let me share with you the three types of tutors: (1) homework tutor, (2) instructional tutor, and (3) strategic tutor.

Three Types of Tutors

Homework Tutor	Instructional Tutor	Strategic Tutor

The Homework Tutor

This type of tutoring requires the tutor to research all the client's school information to help him or her successfully. This information includes teacher information, current grades, and assignment calendars depending on the grade level. Parents sign a release form allowing you, the tutor, to gain access to grades and contact teachers. Please keep in mind that some school districts require that the parents submit a written request to allow a tutor to communicate with teachers about academic matters, such as homework, tests, and projects. To protect yourself and your business, please make sure that you have written consent, as well as your own consent form for clients to sign, especially if you are dealing with children under eighteen or with special needs.

If you are lucky enough to start working with clients at the beginning of the school year or semester, this type of tutoring will seem easy to you. In this case, it is important for you to help the student organize his or her binders or course material for easy navigation.

For example, a client may have a math class binder that needs sections labeled:

TAB 1

TAB 2

TAB 3

TAB 4

TAB 5

Second, the tutor should set personal-learning goals for each tutoring session. I have noticed that clients tend to do a better job when they have a written agreement that can be referred to from time to time. Ultimately, the goal for each client should be to improve his or her skills.

Third, the tutor should set mini-goals to be achieved for each session. For example, if you are working with a client for at least three days, it will be a good idea to have a weekly schedule so that you and the client (and the parents) are fully aware of these sessions.

SCENARIO:
"Not Another Missing Assignment!"

Isabella, a seventh-grade student who is gifted in mathematics, has ADHD and an information-processing disorder. Her parents notice that she has low grades in all her subjects and cannot turn her assignments in on time because her homework is either incomplete or lost. Isabella's parents become frustrated and hire a tutor who can help Isabella with her homework. The tutor's name is Renee.

Renee takes the position (a new way of tutoring for her) and immediately starts working with Isabella. She and Isabella meet three times a week on Tuesdays, Thursdays, and Saturdays. During the first session, Renee realizes that she does not have a clue about Isabella's class assignments and when assignments are due. The only information that is available to her is the assignments that Isabella brought to the session, which is frustrating. This is Renee's first experience being a homework tutor, so she is a little hesitant to ask the parents for more information.

After two weeks, Isabella's situation still does not change—there are still several missing assignments and her grades only improve a little. At that time, Renee has a conference with the parents and asks if she may have permission to contact teachers and/or have access to Isabella's grades. The parents agree to give Renee full access to Isabella's grades, which can be accessed online, since the school district had implemented an online grade book system so that parents are informed about their child's grades in school.

At the end of the grading period, Isabella's grades have improved in all her classes, and she has been missing fewer assignments, thanks to Renee's ability to access her grades in a timely fashion. Also, Renee recommends that she visit with Isabella three times a week, preferably on Tuesdays, Thursdays, and Sundays or Mondays, Tuesdays, and Thursdays. Renee knows that she can better assist Isabella if they meet on those days and have 90-minute or 120-minute sessions.

1. How do you deal with clients who need help with homework and organizational skills?

2. How would you have explained to Isabella's parents the importance of keeping Renee up-to-date with her studies?

> **Expert's Advice:** As a homework tutor, you will need to have full access to your client's grades. It would help if parents give you written permission to communicate with the student's teachers. I must forewarn you that most parents will only give you access to grades, and that is fine. Your main focus should be to help the student set weekly and six-week goals to get his or her homework turned in on time and improve his or her grades.
>
> If parents will not give you access to their child's grades or provide a copy of the current grades prior to the tutoring sessions, I strongly encourage you to think twice about accepting the tutoring position. This type of uncooperation

> **Expert's Advice** *(continued)*
> will do a disservice to the client and can tarnish your business image or reputation. I have had two clients for whom I was a homework tutor. One client's parents gave me full access, while the other client's parent did not. Therefore, I have learned to implement guidelines for clients when they come to me for homework or study skills assistance.

The Instructional Tutor

The instructional tutor is a tutor who plans instruction according to the client's needs; tutoring lasts anywhere from six weeks to eight months. This type of tutor works with clients who need a minimal amount of assistance on homework. Oftentimes this type of tutor develops an instructional plan to work on skills that need further attention and supplement a student's classroom experience. Most tutors will be this type of tutor. They will learn a lot about their clients because they will be working with the client for at least six weeks at a time. Again, this depends on the client's needs and the instructional plan.

A typical session with an instructional tutor will last thirty minutes to two hours and will follow the same structure as all sessions. You may, however, want to differentiate how the session time is used. For example, for math and science sessions, you may want to schedule at least forty-five minutes to sixty minutes, while an English Language Arts (ELA) session will be ninety minutes to allow for both a reading and writing session. In any event, this type of tutoring will resemble classroom instruction and will hone your teaching/tutoring skills. If you are deciding to enter the classroom or refine your tutoring skills, then this type of tutoring will help you achieve your desires.

SCENARIO: *"I'm So Glad We Found You!"*

Mahogany Nicole, a physically disabled and hearing-impaired fourth grader, needs help in math has been in and out of school due to her medical conditions since first grade. Her parents have tried helping her and now that she has been promoted to fifth grade, they are looking for a qualified tutor who can help her. Mahogany's dad saw an ad on the bulletin board at a local grocery store and decided to call Kendall, the math tutor who had posted the listing. Kendall asked the parents a series of questions and informed them that she would have to administer a diagnostic assessment prior to working with Mahogany. She also asked them whether they could bring a copy of her Individual Education Plan (IEP) and other academic records.

At the tutoring consultation, Mahogany took the diagnostic assessments, and Kendall told the parents that the next step would be to create an instructional plan for Mahogany. Based upon the diagnostic assessments, it was clear that Mahogany would need at least six weeks of tutoring (twice a week) to cover the gaps from second to fourth grade and work on the fifth- grade concepts. The parents agreed to the instructional plan and prepaid for both the tutoring consultation and the first six sessions. Mahogany's parents signed a payment agreement stating that the remaining amount would be paid before the seventh tutoring session. The following Monday, Mahogany and Kendall began their first session.

1. Do you think that this is the ideal client for whom Kendall should work? Why or why not?

_____
_____
_____
_____

2. What additional marketing strategies would you employ to strengthen Kendall's marketing plan? If you would not change anything, why is that so?

_____
_____
_____
_____
_____

The Strategic Tutor

A strategic tutor works with clients who need academic assistance for less than six weeks. In order to serve as a strategic tutor, you must be extremely organized and know which approach to take with each client. As a strategic tutor, it's imperative to have the client complete a pre-assessment. This pre-assessment will give you a better picture of how the client is currently performing in that specific area. In addition to the pre-assessment, it's important to have any school-related data that will provide a history of the client's educational background. Later in this book, you will learn exactly how to develop a pre-assessment or locate one using the Internet.

SCENARIO: "Last-Minute Help"

Sebastian, an undergraduate college student majoring in business, needs to take one course in order to graduate at the end of the semester. He had to take the college entrance exam and failed it by thirty points. Sebastian found out that he needed to improve his college algebra and score a higher grade in order to get into the college algebra course. He started desperately looking online for a tutor because he would take the test again in three days and the class started the following Monday.

He did not have a lot of money, so he was looking for someone who was affordable yet knowledgeable and could help with his immediate math needs. He tried calling several tutors, but only one tutor was available; his name was George. George was booked, but he made time for Sebastian.

Prior to the session, George asked Sebastian to bring his score report and any study material that he had been using. Once he had access to this information, he began to formulate a plan. While the college math course placement exam focused on higher math (calculus, trigonometry, etc.), it was smarter to focus on the basic math and progress to the college algebra. Therefore, George designed mini-lessons that mainly covered college algebra but also had to include the basic math so that the client could understand why the process was needed. In other words, it was equally important to cover the basic math concepts so that the client could understand how some of the mathematical processes at a higher level worked and how they built upon the basic mathematical concepts. After a couple of two-hour sessions, Sebastian had acquired all the skills he needed to be proficient, and time had run out for him—the test was the next day.

George was concerned because he knew that more sessions were needed. The following week, Sebastian called George to tell him that he had scored high enough to be eligible to take his college algebra class and would be graduating soon. Sebastian thanked George for making time for him and said that he would come again or recommend him to others. George was extremely happy and realized that he might be able to do it again with other clients.

•••

1. If you were in this situation, would you have serviced this client? Why or why not?

_____
_____
_____

2. If you could interview George, what type of questions would you ask him? Why?

> **Expert's Advice:** I would not recommend that tutors take on a tutoring job like this unless they are sure that they can fulfill the client's needs. If so, these types of jobs will boost your reputation and clientele. Also, you will find that a lot of clients will come to you at the last minute for test prep. If you can successfully help clients at the last minute, you will be accomplished as a tutor—just don't forget to write down your strategies to refine them for the next client who may need assistance with the same test or skill.

Tutoring Archetypes That Work Best with High School and Adult Learners

Harootunian and Quinn (2008) identify and describe three tutor archetypes: (1) the pragmatist, (2) the architect, and (3) the surveyor (p. 15). These tutor archetypes are commonly used with high school and adult learners, but, depending on your teaching style, you may be able to incorporate these archetypes with younger learners.

Tutoring Archetypes for High School and Adult Learners

The Pragmatist Tutor	The Architect Tutor	The Surveyor Tutor

The Pragmatist Tutor

"The pragmatist views tutoring as a series of organized events. These type of tutors ask a variety of 'why' questions designed to help tutees [clients] focus on the steps needed to solve the problems," (Harootunian & Quinn, 2008, p. 15). In other words, pragmatist tutors like to have a structured tutoring session. Pragmatist tutors have an objective for the lesson, just like a teacher.

The tutoring styles of pragmatist tutors include the following:

1. Advocates for strong work ethic
2. Favors worksheets and regular practice
3. Uses a questioning technique that involves direct answers
4. Communicates mostly during dialogues with the tutees (Harootunian & Quinn, 2008, p. 16).

This type of tutoring should be limited when conducting tutoring sessions. It focuses on the tutor rather than the client, whereas clients should experience most of the learning process. Harootunian and Quinn (2008) warn, "[P]roviding everything for tutees [doing all the work for clients] is not effective and should be reconsidered" (p.16). In other words, tutors who choose the pragmatist tutoring approach will be doing a disservice to clients and their tutoring business's reputation may be at stake. So, don't jeopardize everything you have worked hard for by being this type of tutor.

SCENARIO: "I'm Still Confused"

Emily, a bona fide tutor, has been tutoring for over ten years. She has mastered being a tutor but has recently noticed declining passing rates for her clients. She believes that learners should figure stuff out for themselves, just like she had to do. At each session, she gives out worksheets and does all the talking during discussion time.

1. How can Emily improve her tutoring sessions?

2. What are some additional strategies that Emily can employ to help with engaging her learners?

Expert's Advice: In Emily's case, she seems to have forgotten what it took to be a well respected tutor. I would recommend that Emily explore or even blend some of the other tutor archetypes to accommodate her clients' needs. By using worksheets and dominating the learning opportunities, Emily is doing an injustice to her clients. While I am not saying those worksheets are "bad," there are so many more strategies that can be used to teach her clients. Emily must not forget that her clients may have a learning style different from her own, and she needs to cater to their needs and not hers.

The Architect Tutor

"The architect views the study of math as finding pieces of information that create the steps necessary to solve a particular problem" (Harootunian and Quinn, 2008, p. 16). In other words, this type of tutor focuses on making sure that the clients understand; then he or she follows up with higher-level questions, such as why, how, and what. The tutoring styles of architect tutors are the following:

1. Scaffolds [guides] students to help them gain a better understanding, which is followed by strategically crafted questions.
2. Uses diagrams (visuals) to help clients make connections between concepts.
3. Uses questioning strategies that are followed by a new level of inquiry when clients respond.
4. Uses a particular problem-solving style to solve problems.
5. Uses the tutees' responses to determine their learning styles and abilities and conducts sessions in a manner that best supports the client (Harootunian & Quinn, 2008, p. 17).

Although the characteristics of the architect tutor emphasize math, this approach can be applied to any subject. The architect approach lends itself to asking highly effective questions and truly helps clients grasp the material.

Harootunian and Quinn (2008) say it best: "The client's goal in classes is not to get good grades or pass tests, but to learn the material. By setting that as a goal, it then helps him or her achieve the grades and test scores that he or she wants," (p. 17). This description from a client's perspective is powerful, and tutors need to revisit why they chose a certain tutoring approach in the first place.

SCENARIO: "I Got It Now!"

Mercedes, a well respected tutor in her community, accepted a client who needed help with geometry. Joe, the client, did not have anything available to the tutor, other than his grade report. Mercedes asked him what he needed assistance with, and he told her working with right triangles in a problem-solving context. Mercedes knew immediately that he meant trigonometry. She then showed Joe a word problem that contained an image of a right triangle where one leg of the triangle was a flagpole. The question required Joe to find the length from the ground to the top of the flagpole. Once Joe acknowledged that this was the type of question with which he needed assistance, she began to ask a series of questions.

By the end of the session, Joe was working problems independently, but he still had questions about some of the problems. Mercedes continued to ask questions that sparked thinking about how and why he chose to solve the problems the way that he did, while also encouraging Joe to use the visuals provided in the problem or to construct his own. Joe made a three out of four on his mini-assessment at the end of the tutoring session. Mercedes told him to keep up the great work and that he would do fine on this material.

• •

1. What strategies did Mercedes employ in her tutoring session with Joe that made it a successful session?

_____
_____
_____
_____
_____

2. How do you find out what your clients need in such a short time, if an assessment is not given?

_____
_____
_____
_____
_____

3. Do you use the same strategy as Mercedes? Why or why not?

___

> **Expert's Advice:** Mercedes provided a tutoring environment that allowed her client, Joe, to feel comfortable to make mistakes, yet she asked effective questions that guided him in the right direction. Mercedes knew that Joe had background knowledge with right triangles, but she helped him think about everyday objects and how they relate to some aspect of math. Joe had to make a visual image of how a flagpole may look; this visual helped him understand how to solve problems and use common sense to answer the problem. I believe that Mercedes' approach to tutoring helped her client. These strategies were definitely data-driven and catered to the client. Did you notice that Mercedes used a worksheet to assess Joe's needs? In this setting, worksheets are fine because you need to have a quantitative measure to assess your client's needs. Most tutoring sessions will require this archetype, especially if you are an instructional tutor. Again, this solely depends on your client's needs.
>
> The bottom line is you must first determine what your clients' needs are and then choose the best tutoring model to fit them. It may be that you have to blend some of the models to meet your clients' needs, so you need to look at all types of tutors and choose carefully.

The Surveyor Tutor

"The surveyor examines a subject's terrain and creates maps, charts, and diagrams to provide his tutees with visual representations of the landscape" (Harootunian and Quinn, 2008, p. 17). In other words, this type of tutor focuses on looking at the big picture of a concept and then makes both a mental map of approaching the concept and a visual for helping clients make sense of the concepts.

The tutoring styles of surveyor tutors are the following:

1. Prefers unstructured tutoring format and lets the tutees' needs and questions guide the direction of the tutoring session.
2. Places greater emphasis on assisting them to discover the correct aspects of math theory to apply to each problem.
3. Concentrates much of his or her energies and talents on figuring things out.
4. Demonstrates a calm demeanor and a willingness to approach each tutoring session as representing a new set of ideas that need to be understood.
5. Uses questions that are open and spontaneous, created to fit the terrain of each learning situation.
6. Engages the tutees in an articulate manner and strives for balance and conceptual understanding, often taking many steps to solve problems.
7. Prefers the team approach to learning (Harootunian and Quinn, 2008, pp. 17-18).

After looking at each type of tutor and the tutoring archetypes, it is very important for tutors to ask themselves how to determine their tutoring purpose for each client. This can be done by assessing the client's needs at the tutoring consultation. That way, you can quickly identify the type of tutor(s) that you may need to be to ensure that the client meets his learning goal(s) while attending your tutoring practice.

In this chapter, you examined the various types of tutors, along with their tutoring styles. Also, you learned that you would need to choose the tutoring model that best fits your tutoring style yet meets the client's needs. Now it's time to take a look at how to conduct tutoring sessions.

Where to Go From Here

Look out for other Dr. Alicia Holland's products and services. You can stay updated by visiting her personal website, www.dr-holland.com. You can also contact her via the contact form on her personal website to request services.

Should you have questions or comments, suggestions for future material, or tips, feel free to email her at: drhollandj@thetutoroutreach.com.

Join our Membership Group

Visit www.myonlinetutoringbusinessblog.com to gain access to exclusive content and interact with Dr. Alicia Holland so that you can strategically move your tutoring business from good to great.

Last but not least, if you are interested in networking with like-minded tutor business owners, join our FREE Closed Facebook Group—My Online Tutoring Business.

Our Closed Facebook Group is growing fast and group members are eager to connect with you and share their tutoring experiences with you. We truly have what you would call a Professional Learning Community.

Until next time, Happy Tutoring!

Reference

ATA (American Tutoring Association). 2012. About ATA. Retrieved August 6, 2012, from http://www.americantutoringassociation.org/

ATP (Association for the Tutoring Profession). 2012. The history of the Association for the Tutoring Profession. Retrieved August 6, 2012, from http://www.myatp.org/

Bray M. and Silova, I. (2006). The private tutoring phenomenon: international patterns and perspectives, Education in a Hidden Marketplace: Monitoring of Private Tutoring, Overview and Country Reports. Open Society Institute, New York.

EIA (Education Industry Association). 2012. Overview of the education industry association. Retrieved August 6, 2012, from http://www.educationindustry.org/tier.asp?sid=1

Gonzalez-Mena, J. 2009. Child, family, and community: Family-centered early care and education. Upper Saddle River, NJ: Pearson.

Harootunian, J., and Quinn, R. 2008. Identifying and describing tutor archetypes: The pragmatist, the architect, and the surveyor. The Clearing House, 82(1), 15-19.

ITA (International Tutoring Association). 2012. About ITA. Retrieved August 6, 2012, from http://www.itatutor.org/about.php

Holland, A. (2010). *Becoming a Better Tutor: A Data-Driven Approach to Tutoring. 1st Edition.* Bloomington, IN: iUniverse.

Merriam-Webster Online Dictionary. 2012. What is tutoring? Retrieved July 27, 2012, from http://www.merriamwebster.com/dictionary/tutoring

Merriam-Webster Online Dictionary. 2012. Definition of praise. Retrieved June 26, 2012, from http://www.merriam-webster.com/dictionary/ praise

NTA (National Tutoring Association). 2012. Welcome to NTA. Retrieved August 6, 2012, from http://www.ntatutor.com/

About the Author

Dr. Alicia Holland is one of those rare people who can say she is an educator, professional tutor, instructional designer, curriculum developer, online professor, life coach, consultant, speaker, and author and mean it. She started her teaching career at the age of 20 and later earned her doctorate degree in Education from Nova Southeastern University in Ft. Lauderdale, Florida in 2010 at the age of 26. Her God-Given talents and skills have attracted clients such as school districts throughout the United States, state agencies, and other leading learning organizations, including in the private sector.

Dr. Holland consults with tutors and other learning organizations both large and small. Her tutoring blog for tutors has been online since 2010 and she coaches tutors around the world. Typically, she speaks at major conferences each year on topics in education, including tutoring. Dr. Holland is an online associate faculty member at Concordia University Portland where she teaches doctoral level organizational leadership and writing courses in the School of Education.

Also, Dr. Holland has held appointments as an online professor at Ashford University, American College of Education, and Everest Online where she served in the capacity of Internship Supervisor for Bilingual and English Language Learner Educators and taught various courses in Education, Life Skills and Critical Thinking. Additionally, at Capella University, in the Graduate School of Education, she taught various courses in Education and currently serves as a Dissertation Mentor for Doctoral Learners. Lastly,

Dr. Holland teaches doctoral level research courses and serve as either Dissertation Chair or Committee Member at the University of Phoenix. Currently, she is serving as a Lead Area Faculty Chair in Research and was awarded and recognized as one of the 2016 Research Fellows for her research on *Meditation, Mindfulness, and Critical Thinking*. In July 2017, Dr. Holland and her research team will present the original research at Ryerson University in Toronto, Canada.

Outside of Academia, Dr. Holland is a Transformational, Intuitive Life Coach and Ordained Spiritual Minister. In September 2016, she presented her personal development presentation, *Changing Your Client's Story through Personal Power* at Harvard University in Boston, Massachusetts. In November 2017, Dr. Alise will be in Paris, France (City of Love & Freedom) sharing research on *"Integrating Flower Essences Therapy and Intuition in Life Coaching"* at the 8th International Conference on Traditional & Alternative Medicine.

When Dr. Holland is not developing new content, life coaching, tutoring, teaching, or consulting with her clients, you can usually find her sight-seeing and spending quality time with her family enjoying the Desert Sunrises and Sunsets.

Index

A

Adult learners
    architect tutors, 146-148
    homework tutors, 135-139
    instructional tutors, 135, 139-141
    pragmatist tutors, 144-145
    strategic tutors, 135, 141-143
    surveyor tutors, 149-150
    tutoring archetypes that work best, 143-144
Advertising, 50-51. *See also* **Marketing strategies and issues**
Agreements with clients regarding sessions, 60-64
Archetypes of tutors, 135-150. *See also* **Adult learners**
Architect tutors, 146-148
Attendance reports in online tutoring platforms, 42
Attitude and effort, monitoring notes, 83
Automobile insurance, budgeting, 33

B

Billing up front, 64
Book or e-book, complimentary, 72
Branding, 20-21
Budgeting, 27-35
    décor of office, 29
    furniture, equipment, and supplies, 29
    insurance, 33
    marketing, 30-31
    office space, 29-30
    office supplies, 27-30
    outsourcing, 33-34
    payroll and taxes, 31-32
    professional development, 34-35
    savings regimen, 30
    software, 28-29
    taxes, 31-32
    technology equipment and supplies, 28-29
    travel, 34
Business cards, 26, 70
Business name, 20-23
Business structure, 23-25

C

Chamber of Commerce, joining, 54
Chat feature in online tutoring platform, 40, 44
Clients
    agreements, 60–64
    assistance with first session, 73
    billing up front, 64
    discounts, offering, 64
    in-take form, 56
    scheduling for online tutoring, 66–68, 72
    scholarships, providing, 56–58
    welcome packets, 69–73. *See also* **Welcome packets.**
    working with, 54–74. *See also* **Working with new and returning clients.**
Compensation, budgeting, 31–32
Complimentary book or e-book, 72
Computers and supplies, 28–29
Conducting online tutoring sessions, 75–85
    arrive early, 75–76
    monitoring notes, 81–85
    program settings, 77
    sample closing of session, 79–80
    sample opening of session, 77–79
    structure of sessions, 80–81
    technical difficulties, 77
    uploading files, 77
    warm-up questions, 76–77
    welcome message, 76
Conferences, budgeting, 35
Contact information
    website page, 53
    welcome packets, 72
Continuing education courses, 34–35
Contractors, budgeting, 33–34
Corporate identity package, 25–26
Craigslist, 50

D

Décor of office, 29
Direct mailing, 54
Discounts, offering, 64
Dr. Holland-Johnson's Lesson Framework, 95-98
Dr. Alicia Holland's Tutoring Framework, 109-112
Dropbox, 74

E

Effective tutoring, 95-98
Effort and attitude, monitoring notes, 83
E-learning programs. *See* **Online tutoring platforms.**

F

Files
    ability to view and send in online tutoring platforms, 42
    uploading in virtual classroom, 77
Franchise tax, 31
Furniture, 29

G

Google docs, 74

H

Holidays, 70–71
Home page of website, 53
Homework tutors, 135-139
Hours of operation, 70

I

Insurance, budgeting, 33
Instructional tutors, 135, 139-141
International Tutoring and Teaching Symposium, 12

L

Lesson Framework, 95-98. *See also* Dr. Holland-Johnson's Lesson Framework.
Liability insurance, 33
Limited liability companies (LLCs), 23–25
Log-ins
    features in online tutoring platforms, 43
    welcome packet information, 72
Logo, 25–26

M

Marketing strategies and issues, 49–54
    basic strategies, 50–54
    budget, 30–31
    Chamber of Commerce, joining, 54
    direct mailing, 54
    local advertising, 50–51
    logo and corporate identity package, 25–26
    networking, 51
    online advertising, 50
    promotional products, 54, 72
    sponsorships, offering, 52
    strategies, 31
    website, 52–53
Media in online tutoring platforms, 41
Mission statement, 19–20

Monitoring notes, 73–74, 81–85
    attitude and effort, 83
    components, overview, 82
    learner's progress, 83–84
    next instructional steps, 84
    purposes, 81–82
    student and session information, 82–83
    tutor observations, 83
    tutor recommendation, 84
    tutor's rating of session, 84–85
    vocabulary, 83
Monthly newsletters, 72

N

Name of business, 20–23
Networking, 51
Newsletters, 72
Next instructional steps, monitoring notes, 84
"No shows," 66–67

O

Office furniture, 29
Office space
    budgeting, 29–30
    furniture, equipment, and supplies, 29
Office supplies, 27–30
Office technologies, budgeting, 28–29
Online learning organization, developing
    business name, 20–23
    chat only, 44
    conducting online tutoring sessions, 75–85. *See also* **Conducting online tutoring sessions.**
    marketing, 49–54. *See also* **Marketing strategies and issues.**
    online tutoring platforms, 37–47. *See also* **Online tutoring platforms.**
    organizational needs, 49–74
    vision and mission statement, 19–20
    working with new and returning clients, 54–74. *See also* **Working with new and returning clients.**
Online tutoring platforms, 37–47
    attendance reports, 42
    both platform and tutors offered by vendor, 45–46
    chat feature, 40
    features, 40–43
    files, ability to view and send, 42
    group participant features, 42–43
    guidelines for selecting, 37–43
    media, 41
    proprietary software, 46–47

questions to consider, 38-39
recording feature, 41
sign-in and log-in features, 43
webcam, 40-41
whiteboards, 40
Outsourcing budget, 33-34

P

Parents. *See also* **Clients**
monitoring notes, 74
pre-assessments, discussing, 59-60
surveys of online tutoring programs, 74
Partnerships, 24
Payroll, budgeting, 31-32
Pragmatist tutors, 144-145
Pre-assessments, 58-60
Professional development, 34-35
Professional liability insurance, 33
Program survey, 71
Promotional products, 54, 72
Proprietary online tutoring platforms, 46-47

R

Recording online tutoring sessions, 41, 73

S

Sales and use tax, 31-32
Sales copy/brochures, 70
Sample opening and closing of online tutoring session, 77-80
Saving a percentage of income, 30
Scheduling client for online tutoring, 66-68, 72
Scholarships, providing, 56-58
Services page of website, 53
Session links, 72
Sign-ins
features in online tutoring platforms, 43
welcome packet information, 72
Software, 28-29
Sole proprietorships, 24
Sponsorships, offering, 52
Starting your business, 19-35
budgeting, 27-35
business structure, 23-25
corporate identity package, 25-26
logo, 25-26
marketing, 25-26, 30-31
vision and mission statement, 19-20

Strategic tutors, 135, 141-143
Surveyor tutors, 149-150
Structure of online tutoring sessions, 80–81
Student Learning Plans (SLPs), 72
Surveys of online tutoring programs, 71, 74

T

Taxes, 24, 31–32
Technical difficulties during online tutoring session, 77
Technical support for clients, 72
Technology equipment and supplies, budgeting, 28–29
Travel budget, 34
Tutoring Framework, 109-112
Tutoring Framework for Effective Tutoring, 109-112. *See also* **Tutoring Framework**. *See also* Dr. Alicia Holland's Tutoring Framework.
Tutoring Lesson Framework for Effective Tutoring, 95-98. *See also* **Lesson Framework**. *See also* Dr. Holland-Johnson's Lesson Framework.
Tutoring sessions. *See* Conducting online tutoring sessions
Tutors
    assignments, 64–66
    conducting online sessions, 75–85. *See also* **Conducting online tutoring sessions.**
    monitoring notes, 73–74, 81–85. *See also* **Monitoring notes.**
    "no-show," 66–67
    observations, monitoring notes, 83
    surveys of online tutoring programs, 74
    vendor of online tutoring platform, offering, 45–46

V

Video clips in online tutoring platforms, 41
Vision of business, 19–20, 21, 23
Vocabulary, monitoring notes, 83

W

Warm-up questions, 76–77
Webcam, online tutoring platforms, 40–41
Website
    company's blog, 73
    as marketing strategy, 26, 31, 52–53
Welcome message in virtual classroom, 76–77
Welcome packets, 69–73
    business cards, 70
    complimentary book or e-book, 72
    contact information, 72
    holidays, 70–71
    hours of operation, 70
    monthly newsletters, 72

        program survey, 71
        promotional products, 72
        sales copy/brochures, 70
        session links and log-in information, 72
        Student Learning Plans (SLPs), 72
        technical support information, 72
        tutoring schedule, 72
        welcome letter, 70
        what client can expect, 71
        white paper, 71
Whiteboards in online tutoring platforms, 40
Worker's compensation liability insurance, 33
Working with new and returning clients, 54–74
        13-step process, overview, 55
        assisting client with first session, 73
        billing up front, 64
        client agreement regarding sessions, 60–64
        client in-take form, 56
        discounts, offering, 64
        monitoring notes from tutors, 73
        monitoring sessions and progress, 73
        pre-assessment, 58–60
        scheduling client for online tutoring, 66–68, 72
        scholarships, providing, 56–58
        tutor assignments, 64–66
        welcome packets, 69–73
Workshops and conferences, budgeting, 35

www.ingramcontent.com/pod-product-compliance
Lightning Source LLC
Chambersburg PA
CBHW070553160426
43199CB00014B/2487